To The Villanuevas~

Here's to many, many
wonderful years in your
beautiful new home. We're
so happy to be able to
visit whenever we feel the
needs to see our favorite people!
Your neighbors~
The Jewells
April 2000

THE

ARTS & CRAFTS

HOME

THE ARTS & CRAFTS HOME

KITTY TURGEON

ROBERT RUST

FRIEDMAN/FAIRFAX
PUBLISHERS

To our families and to the extended family
of the Roycroft Renaissance, who have
encouraged and supported our passion for
Arts and Crafts.

©1998 by Michael Friedman Publishing Group, Inc.

Library of Congress Cataloging-in-Publication data available upon request.

ISBN 1-56799-455-5

Editors: Susan Lauzau and Elizabeth Helfgott
Art Director: Jeff Batzli
Designer: Howard P. Johnson
Photography Editor: Wendy Missan
Production Manager: Susan Kowal

Color separations by Radstock Repro Ltd.
Printed in England by Butler & Tanner, Ltd.

1 3 5 7 9 10 8 6 4 2
For bulk purchases and special sales, please contact:
Friedman/Fairfax Publishers
Attention: Sales Department
15 West 26th Street
New York, New York 10010
212/685-6610   FAX 212/685-1307

Visit our website:
http://www.metrobooks.com

ACKNOWLEDGMENTS

It has been a lifelong dream of ours—one of us an interior designer, the other an art historian—to write about the ideals and style of the international Arts and Crafts Movement and include the current Arts and Crafts Revival. Robert and I were delighted to have been able to assemble over the past dozen years a shop full of Roycroft and other authentic Arts and Crafts furniture and accessories, creating The Roycroft Collection, but to be able to share our knowledge by writing books has been the best reward.

We appreciate our Roycroft Shop's managers, Robert's sister Suzanne Crotty and Theresa Brenner, who have minded the store while we took time off to write this book. We are grateful to Tisha Zawisky, the assistant director of the Foundation for the Study of the Arts and Crafts Movement at Roycroft for not only taking on more of that responsibility, but also for her word processing of some of the numerous drafts and doing much of the research to produce the chronology, biographies, and resource guide.

We also want to thank our former assistant and newsletter editor Ann Haselbauer (who is now in law school). Ann has helped rearrange words to eliminate dangling participles and split infinitives and has corrected punctuation, spelling, and run-on sentences.

I am very appreciative of the many hours my daughter Gillian Turgeon spent on this project, first deciphering my handwriting and then questioning our interpretation of the Arts and Crafts Movement's history and renaissance. This helped us give up unneccessary scholarly detail in return for a clarity that will appeal to beginners and the initiated alike. We spent some great quality time together.

I guess I owe a certain amount of gratitude to my Arts and Crafts front porch where I wrote during the summer of 1997.

Both Robert and I want to thank our editor Susan Lauzau and developmental editor Liz Helfgott for their input and final editing but even more for first leaving us alone at our own pace to do the work. Robert's skill at choosing the right photographs and picking out the pertinent details for captions could not have been done without Wendy Missan's sleuthing all the good photos from which to choose. We are indebted to everyone at Friedman/Fairfax Publishing and especially to the book's designer, Howard P. Johnson, for making our thousands of words look so good. We are certainly proud to put our names on *The Arts & Crafts Home*.

FOREWORD

IN RECENT YEARS, as historians have researched the Arts and Crafts era, some important new information about the philosophy and style has become available. One of the most influential ideas to come to light is the discovery that the American Arts and Crafts Movement was not a return to pure handcraftsmanship but rather a move toward holistic values. Instead of strictly re-creating the methods of times past, Arts and Crafts proponents advocated a back-to-basics philosophy that allowed them to enjoy the conveniences of the late nineteenth and early twentieth centuries. The movement celebrated the joys of the simple life, when families were intact and honest craftsmanship and farming gave dignity to every person. However, it also embraced innovations that improved the quality of life, such as electricity and indoor plumbing. A lifestyle that combined the best of new and old emerged, and these ideals were incorporated into thousands of affordable new homes for the growing middle class.

The post-Victorian lifestyle that swept two continents centered around simplicity in both design and life. In England, however, the furnishings that the Arts and Crafts reformers advocated were available only to the wealthy; the common folk who were intended to benefit from the movement could not afford the handcrafted, quality designs. When American entrepreneurs returned from England, where they absorbed the new philosophy and were exposed to new designs in furnishings, they chose to take a different direction. Elbert Hubbard returned to East Aurora to set up a printing operation, founding the Roycroft Press in 1895. Gustav Stickley, after his trip abroad, went home to Syracuse to make furniture at Craftsman Workshops and then to publish *The Craftsman* magazine.

The Americans' decision to embrace the machine—which was essentially a business decision—changed history. Ladies' magazines, along with Roycroft's *Philistine* and *Fra* publications and Stickley's *Craftsman,* launched an enormous marketing campaign to persuade Americans to buy quality machine-made items. The power of the press demonstrated itself, and the Arts and Crafts Movement became far more widespread in North America than anywhere else in its appeal to the middle class.

In 1995, when the Los Angeles County Museum of Art launched its exhibition *Virtue in Design,* it sent a message that changed the perspective of seasoned Arts and Crafts enthusiasts. This daring exhibit revealed the Arts and Crafts Movement as a giant public relations promotion and marketing campaign that created its own identity and marketplace. The traveling show, which featured an accompanying catalogue by Leslie Bowman, inspired other catalogues, lectures, and exhibits, including *Roycroft Desktop; Head, Heart and Hand; Living the Good Life: California Arts and Crafts;* and *The Ideal Home.*

Today the middle class is shrinking and multitudes have been disenfranchised. Too many are left behind by unemployment or underemployment, unable to afford their own homes and less in control of their own destinies. It seems that divorce has helped to splinter the ideal family. Perhaps these issues have helped to ignite the Arts and Crafts Revival, which is in full swing today.

While there have long been true Arts and Crafts enthusiasts who have studied the philosophies and become serious collectors, there are now thousands of novices who love the Craftsman look but cannot afford or find sought-after antiques. These new enthusiasts are delighted to learn that appropriate furnishings, including good reproductions, are just fine whether handcrafted or machine-made. Quality is what counts.

In fact, the most significant trend to surface in the Arts and Crafts Revival has been the acceptance of reproductions, including those made in factories. The realization that many of the original North American Arts and Crafts goods were manufactured by machine in the early twentieth century has resulted in a new respect for current factory-made pieces.

The conferences and symposiums, lectures that complement exhibitions, and exhibition catalogues have all contributed to the Arts and Crafts Revival. Books and magazines devoted to the Arts and Crafts style continue to appear, satisfying the enthusiasts' thirst for information and decorating ideas, and drawing in a whole new audience that is captivated by the beautiful simplicity of the style.

A bonus to those of us working at Roycroft has been to see the image of Elbert Hubbard elevated from a commercial ad man of the Arts and Crafts Movement to its hero, who was able to spread the ideal and make his business a success. Hubbard was a marketing genius who persuaded a generation to choose a simple and informal lifestyle. He and the Roycrofters promoted this theme and then delivered the goods. They understood that handicraft was admired and respected but rarely profitable. Rather than making handcrafting the only and ultimate criterion, they relaxed the earlier standards and allowed a desire for well-made furnishings in a comfortable home to become their guiding principle.

We can applaud the Arts and Crafts Movement and its greatest success—their marketing campaign. Successful marketing itself is an art and a craft. The affordability of the houses and furnishings made that success possible; bungalows and other Arts and Crafts houses were designed to appear larger than they were, and both the houses and the furniture promoted a casual yet elegant lifestyle.

The wide, welcoming front doors of Arts and Crafts houses, their beautiful built-ins, subtle pottery and glass, solid furniture, and exquisite accessories project a message: "Life is good here—we are safe and comfortable, productive and nurtured. Our lives are meaningful." It is a complete picture of the happy home. Who, at the anxious and hopeful beginning of a new millenium, would not wish for the same?

INTRODUCTION

ABOVE: *The Arts and Crafts period signaled a flowering of artistic expression, as shown in this art tile produced by the renowned Rookwood Pottery. Pottery in particular offered opportunities—both creative and economic—for women, who had limited entry into the professional world.*

━━━ ⊡⊠⊡ ━━━

PRECEDING PAGES: *Furnishings of utility and good design—what William Morris called "the beautiful necessities"—were at the very heart of the Arts and Crafts Movement. This substantial collection of Arts and Crafts furniture and accessories lends character to a well-lit modern space. Both original pieces and fine reproductions make handsome additions to every home.*

━━━ ⊡⊠⊡ ━━━

MORE THAN A DECORATING STYLE, Arts and Crafts is a celebration of quality, integrity, and simplicity, in both life and design. Though this marriage of philosophy and style has its origins in the mid-nineteenth century, the finely crafted furniture, subtly colored pottery and textiles, and handsome mica-shaded lamps have made a spectacular comeback, and are as fitting in today's homes as they were at the turn of the century.

At the roots of the Arts and Crafts Movement was a desire to return to quality in workmanship and design, and this general principle led to various international and regional interpretations, including Art Nouveau in France, Mission style in North America, the Vienna Secession in Austria, and so on. These styles differ significantly in appearance, but all rely on nature as a source of creative inspiration and use nature's basic elements to achieve integrity in design.

The term "Arts and Crafts" was coined in 1887 by T.J. Cobden-Sanderson, a member of the British Art Workers Guild. The guild was formed 1884 by a group of architects who were concerned that building had lost its artistry and felt that craftspeople needed a forum for their creations. Those working in the fine arts had never embraced artisans, such as furniture makers and bookbinders, as kin. Members of the British Art Workers Guild felt, however, that these more practical arts were as worthy of recognition as painting and sculpture. Using the motto "Unity of Arts," the guild held in 1888 the first exhibition that harmonized "arts" and "crafts," and the Arts & Crafts Exhibition Society was born.

The philosophy of Arts and Crafts also became the creed of a major social reform movement. In the mid-nineteenth century, reformers began reacting against what they considered the dehumanizing effects of the Industrial Revolution. They drew connections between work environments and the ability of workers to contribute positively to their communities, contending that brutal factory conditions led to physical and mental weakness, low production, depression, and even crime. Beautiful surroundings, many argued, would improve the morale of workers, directly benefiting society. The movement also held that pride in work had to be restored: quality and fine design should be emphasized. Arts and Crafts advocates sought to emulate the traditions and work ethic of the medieval craft guilds as a way to combat mass production, shoddy workmanship, gaudy ornamentation, and useless products.

The goal was clear. The crafts worker must also be an artist, or at least artistic enough to transform the designer's concept into a beautiful and functional piece. The items people used every day in their homes and workplaces would be elevated to the realm of art. These beautiful necessities would make society better and happier by encouraging pride of workmanship in the producers and by inspiring joy in the users.

A triumvirate of advocates stands out among the Arts and Crafts reformers: architectural critic A.W. Pugin; philosopher, art critic, and writer John Ruskin; and designer and poet William Morris. Pugin equated a nation's character with its architectural achievements and urged British architects to forsake Greco-Roman styles in favor of Gothic ones. In his writings, Pugin argued that medieval styles were preferable because of their alliance with Christian themes and because of their functional nature. Ruskin, too, embraced medieval architecture, and developed seven principles that he believed structures should embody: Sacrifice, Truth, Power, Beauty, Life, Memory, and Obedience. In his famed work, the *Seven Lamps of Architecture*, Ruskin explained how these qualities were to be expressed by the individuals designing and constructing the building. Morris apprenticed in the office of a Gothic Revival architect, George Edmund Street, though he subsequently turned his attention to painting, wallpaper and textile design, and other decorative arts.

To achieve their vision of a working-class utopia, designers formed ideal craft guilds and artistic communities. Decorative arts societies and companies founded in England in the mid- to late nineteenth century include William Morris & Co. (1861), A. H. Mackmurdo's Century Guild (1882), Charles Robert Ashbee's Guild of Handicraft

BELOW: *This period photograph depicts a quintessential Craftsman interior, the living room at Craftsman Farms, with its exposed log cabin construction and native stone fireplace. Furniture of wicker, leather, and oak is accented with books, textiles, and pottery.*

BELOW: *A Craftsman sideboard designed by Gustav Stickley displays classic Arts and Crafts objects. Hand-hammered copper chargers have acquired a dark patina over time, and complement the copper hardware of the furniture. The natural linen cloth, pewter wine goblets, simple period art pottery, informal flower arrangement, and quartersawn oak sideboard all exemplify the Arts and Crafts ideal of using humble materials and native woods.*

(1882), and the Arts & Crafts Exhibition Society of London (1888). The Chalk & Chisel Club (1895) in Minneapolis was the first Arts and Crafts society in the United States, with the Boston Society of Arts & Crafts following in 1897. The Chicago Arts & Crafts Society was established later that same year, and before the turn of the century guilds and colonies, communities, potteries, and shops were taking on the name and principles of the Arts and Crafts Movement.

From Liberty & Co. in London to Roycroft in East Aurora, New York, the Arts and Crafts Movement was most influential where its business endeavors were commercially successful. The changes brought by the new, improved designs and accompanying work ethic inspired more political goals than the public realized and had a profound effect on social reform. Proponents of Arts and Crafts protested deplorable factory conditions—focusing especially on the plight of children and immigrant women—and drew attention to inhuman labor practices. Inherent in the movement was a belief that to do the "right" thing rather than the "clever" thing should be the ultimate goal; "clever" marketing strategies that called for planned obsolescence were scorned by Arts and Crafts advocates in favor of a basic approach that gloried in sturdy, well-made goods.

JOHN RUSKIN

*J**ohn Ruskin*** (1819–1900), philosopher and art critic, towers above other earlier nineteenth-century influences on art and aesthetics. With several landmark works, Ruskin established design principles that guided architects and designers throughout the Arts and Crafts era. He believed that architecture reflected and influenced the moral fiber of the people who used the structures, and advocated buildings that embodied admirable qualities such as truth, beauty, and power. Ruskin also promoted the idea that craftsmanship and creativity were important for the workers, and pointed to the medieval guilds as a model.

Though Ruskin did not himself design buildings or furniture, his ideals—based on integrity and harmony with nature—were put into practice by his disciple William Morris. Ruskin's influence on the Arts and Crafts Movement extended well into his old age.

A carved polychrome of John Ruskin decorates the wainscot at Little Holland House outside London.

English art periodicals and U.S. ladies' magazines of the 1880s and 1890s played a major role in educating the public about the Arts and Crafts Movement. The *Ladies' Home Journal,* first published in 1883, and, a dozen years later, *House Beautiful,* which began publication in 1896, as well as *The Studio,* from England, and other publications in Europe were instrumental in spreading the new philosophy.

As each country in which the movement thrived was made aware of the new art through magazines, books, and exhibitions, a revolution of sorts began to emerge. While the furniture, pottery, metalwork, and other decorative pieces produced during the Arts and Crafts period may never have been truly affordable for the majority of people, the ideals of quality, craftsmanship, and natural materials spread and were adopted with modifications at all levels of society.

The Arts and Crafts Revival began in earnest in 1972 with an exhibition entitled *The Arts & Crafts Movement in America, 1876–1916*, held at Princeton University. The exhibition traveled to the Chicago Art Institute and to the Smithsonian Institute's Renwick Gallery. This show stimulated an awakening among scholars and experts, and before the decade came to an end an astute group of New York City antique dealers had created a market for Arts and Crafts pieces among an avant-garde looking for interesting undiscovered collectibles. In the 1980s, movie stars and other film personalities found the sophisticated style and holistic philosophy refreshing, and began collecting Arts and Crafts pieces in earnest. By 1990, reproductions of all kinds began to fill the marketplace in order to supply a new generation of Arts and Crafts enthusiasts.

Arts and Crafts ideals and decorating styles resonate at the turn of the millennium as strongly as they did at the turn of the last century. The emphasis on

the peace and nurturing comfort of family and home suits both periods of fin de siècle unease. We are again finding emotional reward in making a house a home, and we have rediscovered the wisdom of the Arts and Crafts Movement. It is essential to our well-being to create attractive and harmonious homes, and this book is meant to help you do just that.

In order to help you better understand the philosophy of nature as style, we've added a background chapter on the history and philosophy of the movement, a glossary of Arts and Crafts terms, a timeline, and a list of Arts and Crafts sites open to

LEFT: *The products of the Arts and Crafts Movement— furniture of fine design and workmanship, handsome lamps that cast a warm glow, and textiles that reflect the themes of nature—are artfully combined in this cozy living room. Here warmth and comfort, the characteristic elements of an ideal home, are represented in the open hearth and the lovely antique Arts and Crafts furnishings.*

visitors. For those who want to learn more about the movement, we have provided a list of other books and periodicals available. Finally, so you can find and buy some of the objects you see, we have provided an extensive resource guide of shops, studios, and artisans selling Arts and Crafts antiques or making Arts and Crafts-style furnishings.

Whether you are an ardent collector who wants to know more about combining your pieces in room settings or a novice decorator who simply wishes to create a home with a touch of Arts and Crafts style, we are confident that the wonderful photographs and text will inspire you to become a true Arts and Crafts enthusiast.

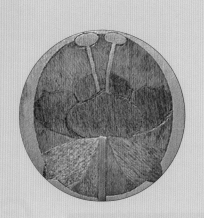

HISTORY
AND
PHILOSOPHY

WILLIAM MORRIS

A period bronze bas relief depicts William Morris during his Kelmscott Press years, 1890 to 1896.

Known as the father of the Arts and Crafts Movement, artist, architect, and designer William Morris (1834–1896) was educated at Oxford, where he met like-minded students Edward Burne-Jones, Gabriel Dante Rossetti, and Philip Webb, who, together with Morris, later became known as the Pre-Raphaelite Brotherhood. Morris studied the philosophies of reformer John Ruskin and developed a deep admiration for the themes and ideals of the medieval period.

Morris & Co. was founded in 1861 to make fabrics, wallpapers, lighting fixtures, and all sorts of furnishings based on the Arts and Crafts principles of simplicity and honesty in design. A lifelong proponent of the Arts and Crafts Movement, Morris possessed a genius for leading and inspiring people that set him above other artists and designers.

foundation of the Arts and Crafts Movement. The house, in Beckley Heath, Kent, was built for Morris and his bride, the beautiful Jane Burden. She was the chief artist's model for the Pre-Raphaelite Brotherhood, as Burne-Jones, Rossetti, Morris, and other of their compatriots became known. Their paintings were stylized renditions of Arthurian legends glorifying medieval myth and high-minded valor. A collection of these paintings at the Delaware Art Museum in Wilmington, Delaware, rivals the holdings of the Victoria and Albert Museum in London. In 1865–67, Morris & Co. was commissioned to decorate the interior of the Green Dining Room at the South Kensington Museum (now the Victoria and Albert Museum), and today, visitors can still view this beautiful space.

SPREADING
THE IDEALS

OTHER LATE-NINETEENTH-CENTURY designers and artisans in England would also further the movement through Arts and Crafts guilds, design firms, craft studios, societies, shops, and larger stores, spreading the holistic philosophy and style to the rest of the British Isles. Harry Clarke of Dublin, Ireland, created mystical stained glass windows, while Hugh Baillie Scott designed quaint cottages on the Isle of Man that were traditionally old world in style but embraced new comforts such as indoor plumbing and electricity. William Burgess,

how the sangreal abideth in a far country
which is sarras the city of the spirit

LEFT: *This exquisite stained glass panel, designed by Edward Burne-Jones and produced by Morris & Co., takes as its subject the secret resting place of the Holy Grail, or Sangreal. Much of the Pre-Raphaelites' work echoes the favorite themes of medieval artists, who were enthralled with the quest for the Grail.*

BELOW: *Arts and Crafts designers were fond of engraving wise words into doors, fireplace hoods, and other surfaces for daily encouragement as well as interior ornament. Here, an epigraph by Walt Whitman adorns the entry door to the reception room of the Roycroft Inn, where many leading lights of the movement met and philosophized.*

designer extraordinaire, redecorated a medieval castle in Cardiff, Wales. Morris and his friend architect C.R. Ashbee resurrected the ancient villages of Burford and Chipping Camden in the Cotswalds. There, in central England, the ancient beauty of yellowed, buttery stone, cobble streets, and church steeples inspired them to preserve buildings, reinvent craft guilds, and write and fight for a new social order.

These Arts and Crafts advocates despised the inhumane labor practices of the mines and factories, and rallied for equal rights and a fair wage for all. Morris defined art as the "expression by man of his pleasure in labor." In art and socialism, he declared, "It is right and necessary that all men have work to do which shall be worth doing and be pleasant to do and which shall be done under such conditions

Produce great people — the rest follows:

CHARLES ROBERT ASHBEE

Charles Robert Ashbee (1863–1942), English architect and designer, studied at Cambridge and went on to design charming houses in the Arts and Crafts style, including his own well-publicized home, the Magpie & Stump.

In 1888 Ashbee founded the Guild of Handicraft, a collective of designers who made furniture, leathercrafts, metalware, and exquisite jewelry. Ashbee's designs for silverware included simple and elaborate pieces often embellished with hammer and wirework, stones, and enamel.

Though Ashbee was initially a purist who believed that handcrafting was the only valid method of producing works, he eventually embraced the machine. This conversion occurred after several trips to America, where he met and befriended Frank Lloyd Wright, whose thoughtful use of machines changed Ashbee's mind on the subject.

as would make it neither over wearisome nor over anxious." Working conditions in general were horrendous, and the message of the Arts and Crafts Movement was a call to fight for human rights. This is once again the cry of a concerned global public at the turn of the millennium, and it has been one of the underlying inspirations for the revival of the Arts and Crafts Movement. We once again appreciate our connection with the planet, evidenced by our concern for the environment and our desire to take personal responsibility for our health.

Members of Ashbee's Guild of Handicraft in England and Elbert Hubbard's Roycrofters in the United States were encouraged to take exercise breaks, and they were fed from the local farm. Both Hubbard and designer Gustav Stickley reported the ills of society in their magazines and promoted the rights of workers, women, and Native Americans.

Hubbard traveled to England to visit Kelmscott Press, established by William Morris, on two occasions in the 1890s. The last endeavor of Morris was to make beautiful books; it became the first of Hubbard's goals, and in 1895 Hubbard borrowed the name Roycroft from two sixteenth-century English printers whose books he collected; the name means Royal Craft, from *roi croft,* or king's farm. He founded the Roycroft Press in East Aurora, New York. Roycroft went on to become a complete enterprise, making furniture and lighting to outfit the growing number of buildings. The company made leather goods as an outgrowth of the printing and bindery. This explosion of the Roycroft enterprise was due in part to the famous essay Hubbard wrote in 1899, "A Message to Garcia." Based on an incident in the Spanish-American War, in which a lieutenant was entrusted with an important message to a Cuban general, the essay was designed to highlight the value of

A B O V E : *Hand-beaten into the copper hood of one of the two fireplaces in the living room at Craftsman Farms is a quote from medieval poet Geoffrey Chaucer—this sentiment underlies the entire Arts and Crafts philosophy.*

ELBERT HUBBARD
AND
ALICE MOORE HUBBARD

The master bedroom of the Scheide-Mantel House, which was built in 1910 by the Roycrofters, is a treasure trove of original dark oak Roycroft furniture (note the distinctive Roycroft orb on many of the pieces). Now a museum dedicated to Elbert Hubbard and Roycroft, the house features a range of vintage furniture and accessories in an authentic setting. Light heart pine flooring, a simple chenille bed-spread, and a Navajo rug accent this classic period room.

Elbert Hubbard (1856–1915) founded the Roycroft in 1895 as a utopian publishing and printing community. While the initial focus was on producing beautiful books, the Roycrofters soon made furniture, stained glass windows, and lighting fixtures, as well as exquisite leatherwork and metalware.

A major advocate of the Arts and Crafts philosophy in the United States, Hubbard was an excellent speaker who lectured throughout the country while Alice (1861–1915) ran the shops. Both Elbert and Alice perished on the *Lusitania*. The Roycroft Inn and Shops, known as the Roycroft Campus, were then successfully run by Elbert Hubbard II, until the campus was forced to close at the end of the Great Depression in 1938. The balance of art, craft, and hospitality made Roycroft the longest-lived and most memorable Arts and Crafts community, and the campus is now a National Historic Landmark.

perseverance and improve morale among workers. Because of its continued popularity, this piece is still in print today, with more than forty million copies circulated in many languages.

Other Arts and Crafts activities followed at Roycroft. Workers began making hand-hammered copper items, such as desk and dining accessories. This craft was an extension of furniture hardware and was an accessory for Roycroft books. Soon catalogues followed, full of all Roycroft's products. Library furniture and accessories became the staple of production. Today, fourteen of the original buildings comprise a National Historic Landmark, and a new era of artisans and shops is flourishing under the banner of a Roycroft renaissance that carries the credo "not as it was then but as Hubbard would do it now."

Fine art and graphic art also are a strong part of Roycroft history. Roycroft's "court painter" was Alexis Fournier, whose newly restored murals once again grace the music salon (now the hotel lobby) of the gloriously renovated Roycroft Inn. The Roycroft community continued to flourish even after Elbert and Alice Hubbard perished on the *Lusitania* in 1915. While the Roycrofters held on throughout most of the Great

ABOVE: *A Prairie-style settle is made comfortable with cushions and pillows decorated with plant and animal motifs. This warm and gracious interior, complete with a tiny Mission-style child's rocker, welcomes visitors to the historic Roycroft Inn. The grand stairway was rebuilt in the 1995 renovation, which restored the Inn to its former glory.*

Depression under the capable leadership of Elbert Hubbard II, called Bert, the company went out of business in 1938. For more than thirty years, Roycroft lay dormant, until, along with the rest of the Arts and Crafts world, it slowly came back to life in what is now a full-blown Arts and Crafts Revival. In decorative arts terms, revivals become official with the prevalence of reproductions that hail a style as a classic.

No other company has added to that current status to the extent of the L. & J.G. Stickley Co., whose Mission oak and cherry collections have helped promote and produce new furniture for Arts and Crafts enthusiasts and Craftsman homeowners everywhere. This current interest in the American version of the Arts and Crafts period extends to the Near and Far East, the British Isles, and Europe.

THE MOVEMENT GROWS IN AMERICA

THE DAWN OF THE twentieth century in the United States found a country in search of an artistic identity. The Arts and Crafts Movement's American style came from a realization that, on the country's hundredth birthday, with its mechanical and industrial skills ahead of the rest of the world, the fine and applied arts were sadly lacking.

OPPOSITE: *Simple without appearing austere, this set of rooms is outfitted in classic Arts and Crafts style. A stenciled frieze incorporates natural themes, bringing the outdoors inside, while such common decorative details as an appliquéd portiere, plain dresser scarf, art pottery, and rugs in earthy colors complement the Craftsman styling of the house.*

Nowhere was this more evident than at the Centennial Exposition of 1876 in Philadelphia, which celebrated the one hundredth anniversary of the signing of the Declaration of Independence. The exposition was international in scope, with forty-nine countries and twenty-six states sending representative works of art and industry. Nearly ten million visitors viewed the mechanical wonders and awe-inspiring designs of every description, including English Arts and Crafts pieces. The exhibition energized American artists, who had the opportunity to see many different styles, not only international, but regional as well. In addition, arts generally thought of as "women's crafts" gained credibility in the art world.

After the Centennial Exhibition, pottery emerged as the decorative art that would lead the way for the Arts and Crafts Movement in the United States. With inspiration from Europe and Asia in the development of glazes and forms, Hugh Robertson started the Dedham Pottery in Boston in 1896, and Rookwood was founded by Maria Longworth Nichols (whose name later changed to Storer) in Cincinnati, Ohio, in 1880. Mary Louise McLaughlin, who in 1879 organized the Cincinnati Pottery club, experimented with glazes that rivaled Haviland in Limoges, France.

Ideals based on wholesome simplicity and a style inspired by nature began to change tastes, and in the reaction to the excesses of Victorian ornamentation a new popular form emerged: the women's magazine. *Ladies' Home Journal* and *House Beautiful* are but two well-known examples of the phenomenon, and Gustav Stickley's *The Craftsman* can be counted among these, as women were among the magazine's most dedicated readers. These "how to" publications presented ideas on fashion, interior decorating, and social issues such as health, schooling, and the simple lifestyle that was proposed at the remedy for the ills of society.

European magazines proliferated and crossed the Atlantic swiftly. *The Studio, Deutsche Kunst and Dekoration,* and *Dekorative Kunst* brought the work of British, Austrian, and German Arts and Crafts architects and designers like Charles Rennie Mackintosh, Hugh Baillie Scott, William Morris, C.R. Ashbee, Kolomon Moser, and Josef Hoffmann to Americans eager for new ideas. And American artists were visiting England and the continent. Both Hubbard and Stickley made trips overseas and returned with a devotion to the movement, merging its principles with American ideals. Stickley redefined the message of British Arts and Crafts proponents, teaching that beauty does not imply elaboration or ornament and that simplicity, individuality, and dignity of effect were important. The beauty of a piece could reside in its superior construction, wood grain, or rich finish. But regardless of how the style was interpreted, one persistent theme remained: all Arts and Crafts designs come from nature.

The Arts and Crafts creed appeared as a talisman against the undesirable effects of industrialization, political corruption of labor, urbanization, and the factory system.

Another fine and influential manufacturer in the United States was Charles Limbert of Grand Rapids, Michigan. He, too, crossed the Atlantic and returned home to

design and produce sophisticated furniture in the fashion of Glasgow's Charles Rennie Mackintosh. Limbert's wonderful cutout tables and chairs are always very high on the list of desirable acquisitions at antiques auctions.

On the West Coast, Henry Mather Greene and Charles Sumner Greene designed what has come to be known as the ultimate bungalow. Frank Lloyd Wright had begun designing his fabulous landmark houses. Dirk Van Erp managed his small metal shop, making the copper and mica lamps that are copied so profusely today. By the turn of the century, the Arts and Crafts Movement was in full swing in North America.

Armed with information about the history, philosophy, and influential figures of the Arts and Crafts Movement, you will better appreciate the care and love that architects, designers, and craftsmen of the era brought to their milieus.

ABOVE: *The extended interior space of the playroom in Frank Lloyd Wright's home shows an appreciation of nature; a gold and green prairie-inspired palette is a stunning backdrop for a wall mural and woodwork in dark, rich tones. The beautiful proportions and simple but stunning interior details, such as built-in bookcases, fireplace, and beamed vaulted ceilings, are typical of Wright's early work.*

CHAPTER

2

ARCHITECTURE:
REGIONAL
INTERPRETATIONS

On both sides of the Atlantic, Arts and Crafts architecture reflects the native materials available and the history that influenced the builders. Lacking a single style, Arts and Crafts architecture instead expressed its designers' object of imbuing the structure with moral character. Simplicity and directness are two qualities valued by architects of the period, who also sought to marry structure to site

and to blur the lines between interior and exterior. A belief in the healing powers of nature resulted in the construction of mountain, country, and seaside homes with architectural styles that made use of the resources of the nearby forests. These woods gave rise to rustic styles such as log cabins and lodges, including shake shingle bungalows.

PRECEDING PAGES: *Traditional English architecture has been translated for this American Arts and Crafts house. The brick foundation is topped by plaster that is accented with timber, a style adapted from Tudor houses. Large art tiles decorated with a grape motif adorn the space below the front windows. Diamond-paned windows on the lower level complete the link to English style.*

LEFT: *This California bungalow is constructed of native stone paired with stucco and dark wood. The house, which seems to grow out of the Pasadena landscape, was designed and built by famed tile maker Ernest Batchelder, who set one of his tiles into the stucco of the chimney.*

GOTHIC
AND
TUDOR STYLES

STYLES BORROWED FROM medieval Continental Europe and England, from lofty castles to quaint cottages, re-created the romance of times past and linked the buildings to a tradition of exquisite craftsmanship. Crenellated towers, Gothic or diamond-paned windows, and rounded rooflines reminiscent of thatched cottages are all Arts and Crafts details borrowed from a bygone era.

The European Gothic churches of the Middle Ages provided much of the original inspiration for Arts and Crafts designers in both England and America. Later, the

OPPOSITE: *Fonthill, the land-mark concrete chateau of tile manufacturer Henry Mercer in Doylestown, Pennsylvania, was inspired by the medieval fortresses of Europe. While the house drew from ancient designs, it was rendered in modern (circa 1910), fireproof material. The house is filled with a fabulous tile collection, some of which was made next door at Mercer's Moravian Tile Works.*

LEFT: *The study at Bok Tower in Florida reflects Arts and Crafts architects' fascina-tion with the Gothic style. The octagonal shape and stunning two-story windows are intended to resemble the interior of a medieval fortress; massive blocks highlight the solid construction demanded in Arts and Crafts buildings.*

ABOVE: *M.H. Baillie Scott's own house on the Isle of Man resembles an old Tudor structure, with its upper story of half-timbered stucco. The colorful bargeboard, decorated with stylized flowers, emphasizes the roofline and adds a touch of whimsy.*

English Tudor Revival houses common in the United Kingdom and New England imitated castles and Tudor fortresses of centuries past.

The first of the buildings constructed by the Roycrofters were simple post and beam structures with plain Gothic windows. The interior of the first print shop at Roycroft was designed in the style of St. Oswald's Church in Grasmere, England. The shop's post and beam construction of natural logs echoes the beautiful church where William Wordsworth is buried. While the interiors and windows of Roycroft buildings had an ancient appearance, some of the exteriors were reminiscent of early New England houses of worship. The print shop, now the Roycroft Inn, has this simple, shake shingle construction.

Hugh Baillie Scott, an architect who worked extensively on the Isle of Man, designed a new prison in 1904 in the town of Castletown that was meant to echo visually the fourteenth-century castle that stood across the street. Similarly, two major edifices at Roycroft, with their crenellated towers of stone and half-timbered construction, were intentionally made to look hundreds of years old, though in fact they were built between 1899 and 1902.

LEFT, TOP: *The crenellated tower of the second Roycroft Print Shop harkens back to the medieval castles of England. Built in 1900 of native glacial stones, this space once housed founder Elbert Hubbard's office and artisan Dard Hunter's studio. The building, which has been in continuous use, stands amid other Roycroft buildings of similar style. Fourteen buildings on the original Roycroft Campus have been designated as National Historic Landmarks.* LEFT, BOTTOM: *The influence of English architecture is clearly evident in the Gothic-style doorway of this Chicago house, designed by Henry Hobson Richardson. The door is flamboyantly embellished with wrought-iron grillwork and medieval-style fittings, which were popular with Arts and Crafts designers.*

SPANISH REVIVAL AND MISSION STYLES

T HE SPANISH REVIVAL houses and public buildings so popular in California and throughout the Southwest were deliberate re-creations of Mediterranean buildings, particularly those found in southern Spain. Characteristics of the Spanish Revival style include stucco walls, wrought-iron grillwork, and glazed accent tiles. These buildings often featured courtyards or other outdoor living spaces that served to link the structures to the landscape and allowed people to take advantage of the warm climate.

Twentieth-century Mission style had earlier origins, arising from the Spanish missions built during the eighteenth century, though the missions themselves borrowed from a more sophisticated Spanish Baroque style.

In fact, the Arts and Crafts Movement helped usher in the preservation movement. The drive to restore the twenty-two missions up the coast of California around 1900 resulted in a new admiration for what has come to be called Spanish-style construction, that is, heavy stucco walls and roofs of adobe tile. Native Americans who lived in these warm climates had realized the practicality of such construction long before the arrival of Europeans, constructing pueblos with thick adobe walls and flat roofs, and those were copied as well.

ABOVE: *Tile insets on building exteriors were a highlight of the Spanish Mission Revival. These green, ocean blue, and cobalt tiles repeat the hues of nature, bringing splashes of color to an exterior without seeming jarring.*
RIGHT: *One strong link to the original California Spanish Mission is the terra-cotta tile roof; these roofs can be found on Spanish-style Arts and Crafts houses throughout North America. The stucco exterior is punctuated by a band of colorful tile, which accentuates the house's horizontal design.*

BUNGALOWS

THE BUNGALOW ORIGINATED IN INDIA, where the "banggolo" or "bangla," an indigenous one-story dwelling, was redesigned by English colonials, who added verandas to shelter them from the sun. European adaptations of bungalows eventually appeared on English seasides and on the seacoasts and lakesides of North America.

Bungalows, as reinterpreted by Arts and Crafts–era architects, come in all sizes, from tiny cottages to the large "ultimate bungalows" designed by Henry Mather Greene and Charles Sumner Greene. Greene and Greene were among those influenced by the austere beauty of Japanese houses. Working extensively in Pasadena, California, in the early 1900s, the pair designed the famous Gamble House, now a museum, as well as the Duncan Irwin, the Freeman Ford, and the Blacker houses, all of which lie within blocks of the Arroyo Seco River. Other architects, also influenced by the Japanese style, included beautiful Asian details in their interior and exterior designs.

ABOVE: *This stunning example of a typical bungalow has several common bungalow features, including exposed rafter tails and large squared porch columns. Symmetrical massing of the house's twin porch entries creates the impression of a much larger house. The decorated triple gables repeat a horizontal emphasis and indicate an Oriental influence.*

RIGHT: *This charming bungalow has the low, sweeping rooflines characteristic of bungalows, but is lacking the classic veranda. Instead, the deep overhang of the roof creates a porch of sorts to the right of the front door, while the house foundation slopes off to the left. The bungalow, as adapted by the English in colonial India, implied a rustic retreat, and this house echoes that impression with its serene setting.*

LEFT, TOP: *The home of architect Charles Sumner Greene in Pasadena shows off its asymmetrical mass and reflects the arroyo environment of southern California. Typical of Greene and Greene's work is the extensive use of wood and exposed joinery, which derived from Japanese styles.*

LEFT, BOTTOM: *The impressive Duncan-Irwin House, designed by Greene and Greene, is one of their "ultimate bungalows." Like other architects and designers of the era, the Greene brothers sought to integrate all aspects of the house, and they designed exterior and interior spaces, lighting, and furniture to work together in an ideal living space. Despite its large size, the balanced scale of the house and its lovely setting give it a homey appearance.*

CRAFTSMAN HOUSES

ABOVE: *This house was designed by Gustav Stickley as a commission from a client. Like many of Stickley's house designs, the plan was later offered to readers in* The Craftsman. *Stickley's blueprints were collected in two books,* Craftsman Homes *and* More Craftsman Homes*, which further popularized his houses.*

GUSTAV STICKLEY'S Syracuse operation was known as Craftsman Workshops, and his Craftsman Home Builder's Club and *Craftsman* magazine, as well as his ideal farm, Craftsman Farms, carried the Craftsman name. Strictly speaking, the only houses that can truly be designated "Craftsman" are those that were built from designs that appeared in the magazine. The floor plans of these homes usually included suggestions for an exterior architectural scheme, offering choices of English Tudor, Spanish Mission, Dutch Colonial, or Bungalow style. Stickley's home, Craftsman Farms, in Morris Plains, New Jersey, is now a National Historic Landmark Museum House. A log structure with a tile roof, the house still sits on a large acreage.

Like many brand names, "Craftsman" became a popular term for all Stickley look-alikes, including both house styles and furniture. In Arts and Crafts Revival nomenclature, "Craftsman" now applies to generic and common copies of Arts and Crafts pieces and architecture. When referring to an item made by Stickley's Craftsman Co., as opposed to a piece made by one of his imitators, it is often identified by enthusiasts as a "Gus" piece. Today the Sears company owns the trademark Craftsman, which is why it is now less associated with Gustav Stickley.

PRAIRIE STYLE

IN THE VAST HEARTLAND of North America, a very different Arts and Crafts style emerged. Characterized by low, nearly flat roofs constructed in sympathy with the unbroken horizon of the Midwestern landscape, these houses usually have deep overhangs and heavy squared columns supporting the porch. Another hallmark of the style is geometric art glass windows, which lessen in some measure the harshness of the houses' lines.

Many of the finest existing examples of this popular Midwest architecture, known as Prairie style, are structures designed by the renowned architect Frank Lloyd Wright. No signature in the Arts and Crafts world is more recognizable than the red square and initials FLW attached to the work of this genius of design. Wright's elegant and magnificent early homes—the Robie, Willits, Dana-Thomas,

BELOW: *One of the earliest Frank Lloyd Wright houses is the Heurtley House, built in 1901 in Oak Park, Illinois. The low-slung roof, wide eaves, recessed windows, and overall horizontal organic form mimic the Midwestern countryside and represent an early example of the Prairie form. The long, thin Roman brick used in the construction is extended for a long garden wall, repeating the house's horizontal theme.*

This Wright-designed dining room shows one of the architect's famous features—the room within a room. High-backed chairs set around a large dining table create a sense of enclosure and intimacy within the larger space.

Today *architect and designer* Frank Lloyd Wright (1867–1956) is lauded as the most profound artistic genius America has produced. He began his career with the firm of Adler and Sullivan, working with Louis Sullivan until 1893. Wright's early houses earned the designation "Prairie style," and his followers, who garnered some of Wright's clients, were dubbed the Chicago School. Wright advocated open-plan interiors fitted with furniture of his own design that was stark and functional with a geometric flair. He designed each house complete with all the interior fittings to complement the building.

Wright was a leading proponent for the change from handcraft alone to machine production, and was among the first in the American Arts and Crafts milieu to welcome use of machines. Like all Arts and Crafts devotees, he embraced simplicity and functionality rather than useless ornamentation that caught the eye but overburdened the mind.

Little, and Martin houses—are classics of Prairie style. Wright proclaimed Buffalo, New York, to be the edge of the American Prairie. There stands the Darwin Martin complex, now under restoration, considered a masterpiece and arguably Wright's finest work of this period. Many architects in addition to Frank Lloyd Wright, including Purcell Emslie and George Maher, designed in the Prairie style, dotting the Midwest and outlying areas with horizontal structures intended to blend into the spreading landscape in the same manner as Wright's houses.

ABOVE: *Wright's proteges used the principles of the Prairie style across North America. The wide, overhangs of this Prairie-style house create shaded environments in summer and well-lit rooms in winter.*

RIGHT: *Typically roomy and rather boxy looking, four-squares are perhaps the simplest to build of all the Arts and Crafts architectural styles. The straightforward lines and practical squared shape of the four-square place it firmly in the realm of "honest" design so prized by Arts and Crafts reformers. This house, located in New York State, incorporates the third-floor dormer common to the style.*

OPPOSITE: *Small but efficient, generally inexpensive yet well designed, the varying architectural styles of the Arts and Crafts era yielded houses that were both affordable and beautifully crafted. Today, many of these sturdy houses continue to offer gracious living to families across England and North America.*

FOUR-SQUARES

ANOTHER ARTS AND CRAFTS style that developed in North America is the large and homely house called the four-square. Two-story, boxy, stable, strong, and useful, the four-square is the practical "Dream House," symbolic of solid values and a prosperous middle class.

This stolid house style is typically found east of the Mississippi and north of the Mason-Dixon line. Its "footprint" is square, and the attic may accommodate dormers and be finished as a third floor. This house's uninspiring shape makes for very efficient use of space and a relatively low cost.

Fascinating is the diversity of the many facades in the Arts and Crafts style. It is important to remember that each region created its own Arts and Crafts architecture, naturally dictated by the plentiful materials and the local approach to glorifying nature and honoring individual heritage.

TYING HOUSE AND LANDSCAPE TOGETHER: PORCHES, PERGOLAS, AND GARDENS

Matching architectural features and landscape is of paramount importance in Arts and Crafts style, and puts the tenets of ecology, regionalism, and unity into practice. The best Arts and Crafts houses include driveways and walkways made of cement, stone, brick, or tile, as well as porches, pergolas, toolsheds, greenhouses, or lattices.

In addition, the featured plants in an Arts and Crafts garden reflect the native character of the surrounding environment, whether it be deep emerald forests, vast fields of wildflowers and grasses, or the subtle beauty of deserts. Because gardens are by their very nature fleeting, few period Arts and Crafts gardens survive, but the writings of garden designers of the day coupled with restored or preserved nineteenth-century gardens allow us to plan a landscape in keeping with the character of an Arts and Crafts house. While it is best to have a complete plan before beginning to work, the landscaping can take place in stages over a period of several years.

PRECEDING PAGES: This magnificent bungalow exemplifies the marriage of house and garden. Though situated on a city street, the landscaping maintains the look of the California scenery.

OPPOSITE: *A lush cottage garden complements Arts and Crafts houses and is achievable in every climate using old-fashioned flowers or native plants. The colorful, informal style is in keeping with the more naturalistic approach to gardening advocated by period garden writer William Robinson in* The Wild Garden. *The pergola, a key feature in Arts and Crafts gardens, links the landscape to the house by virtue of its architectural presence.*
LEFT: *Authentic Arts and Crafts colors on trim and door set the tone for this serene stone porch. By adding an Arts and Crafts–style lantern and a reproduction Adirondack settle with tribal print cushions, this porch is transformed into a comfortable outdoor living space. A touch of greenery beside the door brings the garden right up to the porch.*

FRONT PORCHES

Most ARTS AND CRAFTS HOUSES are tailor-made for romantic porch living. Bungalows, especially, are suited for families who spend much time out of doors, because, by definition, they require a porch. The porch is an invitation to enter, offering a welcoming transition from the street or front garden to the foyer or entryway of the house.

Many Arts and Crafts porches feature heavy squared columns, which ground the structure, conveying a sense of stability and permanence. These supports may be made of wood, stucco, clinker brick, river stones, or any other material that fits the house and its surroundings. Porches vary in size from shallow overhangs that simply shelter the front door from harsh sun or falling rain to spacious outdoor rooms that provide extra living space in nice weather.

RIGHT: *The peristyle—a columned covered walkway— at the Roycroft Inn is outfitted for brunch in warm weather. Fully restored to its original condition, this exterior space is dressed with roman shades that shield diners from the sun. A row of rockers has been painted a few shades darker than the building's trim, a fitting treatment for porch furniture.*

OPPOSITE: *The porch of the Thorsen House celebrates native wood and finely crafted joinery. A floor of brick and terra-cotta pavers recalls the cobbled streets of old cities and continues the natural theme of the space. Amber lanterns contribute a soft glow that mixes beautifully with the muted colors of this open porch.*

Wicker, old or new, is a natural and comfortable way to furnish a porch, but white wicker should be used only if the house trim is white. Glaring white porch furniture on a porch that is otherwise composed of wood tones or subtle colors will destroy the serenity of the space. Note that a bit of rain will not harm wicker; in fact, it requires moisture for flexibility.

A fine idea for furnishing an outdoor room is to use an old rocker painted in the same shade as the house's trim. A porch swing is simply luxurious combined with other pieces painted to match the trim of the house or left with a natural wood finish, and really helps to set a lazy summer day mood.

Fresh flowers such as gladiolas are beautiful when prominently placed "Chatauqua style" (it is the fashion in this landmark community to place large vases of gladiolas on an outdoor table to show that the owner is in residence). These touches contribute an air of elegance to the porch, while attractive floor pots, hanging plants, and wind chimes create a lovely atmosphere. As you shell peas for dinner, entertain friends, read a favorite novel, or write a letter, you'll be wrapped in the comfort of a space well constructed and lovingly decorated. Treat yourself to these relaxing moments often—they create a charming collection of memories in themselves.

RIGHT: *While most original sleeping porches have been turned into extensions of the master bedroom or into second-story decks, a few remain intact. This restored sleeping porch offers healthy "outdoor" sleeping courtesy of banks of windows that virtually surround the bed. The warm look of beadboard paneling reinforces the natural feeling of the room, while a wicker chair, a soft rug, pristine linens, and fresh flowers bring a sense of comfort to the space.*

SLEEPING PORCHES

CHANGES IN LIFESTYLE and new ideas about health that came about toward the end of the nineteenth century greatly affected the design of sleeping areas. Separate sleeping rooms for husbands and wives gave way to the master bedroom during the Arts and Crafts era. Twin beds were common in the master bedrooms of the time, and the acceptability of separate beds in one room gave rise to an alternate summer sleeping arrangement: the sleeping porch.

Special screened-in rooms attached to the bedroom allowed people who lived in the house to sleep virtually out of doors. Unlike people of earlier decades, those living at the turn of the century believed that night air was healthful. Fresh air was thought to benefit the brain and refresh the mind, restoring energy and health to the body. Sleeping porches allowed families to take more of the invigorating air and, in an era before electric fans and air-conditioning, provided a relatively cool spot to rest. Some sleeping porches were so elaborate as to feature a wide door opening off the bedroom that allowed the beds to slide out onto the porch. Mostly, however, sleeping porches were bare rooms either screened or left completely open to the night and furnished dormitory-style with beds where the entire family could slumber. Today, almost all of the original sleeping porches have been enclosed to enlarge the bedroom area. Their transformation into closets or sitting areas further reflects the changing social fabric as expressed in architecture and design.

TERRACES AND COURTYARDS

SOME STYLES OF Arts and Crafts houses are best suited to outdoor spaces such as terraces, courtyards, or patios, while others houses may incorporate both traditional porches and other exterior "rooms." Prairie-style houses for example, generally feature covered terraces on the side or back. English Tudor houses tend to have open terraces, often raised by a stone retaining wall and incorporating steps and a balustrade. Spanish Mission houses, which borrow features from warm-climate traditions, are sometimes "H" or "U" shaped, and center around a courtyard, often with a fountain.

BELOW: *Benches and other outdoor accessories create garden rooms that expand the living area of the home. Even courtyards, terraces, or patios can be planted with specimens that grow well in confined spaces. Here, trees espaliered against a wall soften the solid brick of the structure and add a cooling green to the spot. Flowers planted in unpaved squares offer manageable spaces in which to garden.*

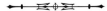

GARDEN FEATURES

WATER IN ANY FORM enhances the landscape. The sound of running water is gently soothing, and filters out noises from traffic or nearby neighbors, helping to create a serene environment. A simple fountain also offers an excellent visual focal point.

Water lily or koi ponds, adopted from Japanese garden tradition, are magical, with or without bridges. Aquatic plants and fish bring a living element into the water garden, and the tiny pond helps render the garden as a microcosm of the world. Still water in pools mirrors the sky and surrounding plants, creating a space that is both literally and figuratively reflective in nature.

No garden structure is as appropriate to the Arts and Crafts style as the pergola, with its open network draped with swaths of flowering vines. Made of wood or

BELOW: *A tangle of greenery frames the view of a castle. The reflective quality of still water enhances every house and garden feature, doubling a beautiful image. The wild garden surrounding this fantastical castle creates an impression of an enchanted place hidden from time.*

sometimes metal, these charming constructions bring architecture into the garden, uniting house and landscape seamlessly.

Walls and fences are lovely accents, as well as practical enclosures if you have children or pets. They can also serve as partial protection from cold and wind for plants overwintering in the garden. When well planned and constructed of beautiful materials, walls and fences provide structure to the garden throughout the year, providing visual interest even in the midst of winter.

Because they are available in a variety of styles and materials, you're almost certain to find a fence or wall that complements the character of your house and garden. Dry rock walls, in which stones and rocks are simply set atop one another, let water drain out of the wall and provide plenty of chinks for growing small rock plants. Mortared stone walls offer a pleasing sense of solidity; although in cold climates they require deep footings, solid walls generally last longer than dry rock walls. Iron fences, alone or set atop brick walls, are elegant and formal, while spaced wooden slat fences are decorative, but a bit more casual.

Arts and Crafts landscape architecture and garden features also include less expensive accoutrements such as sundials, birdbaths, reflecting balls, benches, and arbors. One or more of these lovely accessories will fit into even the most modest space.

Where room permits, a croquet lawn is a wonderful addition. It's lovely to dress in white, sip lemonade, root beer, or something stronger, and gather for a game of croquet. Other lawn games are also suitable, and a tennis court is ideal if one has the ability, space, and budget to make it possible. "Fox in the snow," a labyrinth winter sport, is a family affair that can make the lawn functional year-round. Mazes may be shoveled in new-fallen snow and prizes hidden in the center of the maze.

ABOVE: *A small English fountain adds the soft splashing sound that makes the Arts and Crafts garden such a relaxing retreat. Modest fountains like this one are perfect accents for an Arts and Crafts garden, while large formal examples are often too grand. Fragrant herbs provide the welcome addition of scent to the garden. Consider planting them beside a path where they will be brushed against, which allows them to release their perfume into the air.*

ABOVE: *Electric lanterns were
first used in gardens in the early
twentieth century, and are a favorite garden accent today. This
beautiful Japanese-inspired example serves as both a striking
ornament and practical outdoor
lighting. Set atop a stone retaining wall, the lamp illuminates
the adjacent terrace.*

RIGHT: *An exuberant mix of
flowers, trees, and ferns borders
the path leading to the house,
while a clambering vine nearly
claims the structure as part of
the garden. Unity of house and
garden was a governing principle of Arts and Crafts landscaping, and this concept is as
desirable today as it was a
hundred years ago.*

GARDEN FLOWERS AND VEGETABLES

THE ARTS AND CRAFTS PHILOSOPHY of linking house and site and valuing regional materials extended to the plants used in the garden. The cultivated garden served as a tie between the manmade house and the untamed nature of the surrounding countryside, just as the porch acted as a transition between exterior and interior.

Though the layout of the garden might be geometrical, plantings were rarely so. Arts and Crafts garden designers advocated a return to informal cottage-style plantings, rejecting the Victorian love of "carpet bedding" with showy colorful exotics. Instead, garden designers in the Arts and Crafts mode concentrated on plants that had a history in the area, the flowers planted in the functional but beautiful kitchen and cutting gardens of an earlier era.

BELOW: *Garden designers of the Arts and Crafts era, including renowned plantswoman Gertrude Jekyll, recognized that, though the controlling hand of the gardener might be necessary on a practical level, the designs and color combinations of nature were to be admired as models. In this garden, where order and tumult are carefully balanced, country garden favorites such as climbing roses, lavender, and helichrysum reign supreme.*

OPPOSITE: *Cacti and succulents are native flora of semi-arid climates, and are appropriate to Arts and Crafts gardens in western or desertlike regions. Indigenous plants create an ideal environment for local fauna, attracting the birds, butterflies, and other beneficials that keep a garden healthy and full of life. In addition, plants adapted to a particular region are generally the hardiest choices; this drought-tolerant garden is well-suited to the low rainfall in this part of California.*

The rose is the symbolic flower of the Arts and Crafts era, with unfolding petals representing life's sweetness, and prickly thorns denoting the harsh realities of the world. Roses are among the oldest cultivated flowers, and are associated with English royalty—the White Rose of York and the Red Rose of Lancaster. Nearly every Arts and Crafts artisan has used stylized roses in his or her designs, and the living flower is above all others appropriate to an Arts and Crafts–style garden. There is a full complement of old-fashioned garden roses that were used at the turn of the century and are still available today. Consult one of the many specialty rose books on the market to determine which variety is best for your needs.

There are many other flowers and plants fitting for an Arts and Crafts garden. Sympathetic plants include English cottage garden perennials and bulbs, such as daffodils, violets, tulips, irises, poppies, peonies, delphiniums, foxgloves, lupines, and lilies of all kinds. Once planted, these flowers endure for years, multiplying in size and beauty. Their changing array simultaneously inspires excitement and tranquillity throughout the gardening season.

Flowering climbers and vines like wisteria, clematis, and morning glories are perfect for training on a sturdy pergola. Shrubs and trees that bloom prolifically, if only briefly, such as honeysuckle, forsythia, lilac, and bridal wreath make charming border and perimeter plantings and can be combined to prolong the flowering display. Hedges of privet and boxwood make excellent dividers and screen properties from the view of passersby and next-door neighbors.

Traditional Arts and Crafts landscapes made room for a vegetable, herb, or "sniff and snip" garden (which included annual flowers and herbs for cutting interspersed with berries and vegetables). Apple or pear trees espaliered against a wall or trained as cordons brings luscious fruit as well as beauty to a limited space. Edible flowers, like nasturtiums, chives, and violets, are once again quite fashionable as garnishes.

In addition to old-fashioned favorites, previously overlooked native plants, particularly in North America, were incorporated into Arts and Crafts gardens. This practice is in keeping with the idea of creating a garden to fit the climate and the native flora of the area. It is more appropriate to the Arts and Crafts style (and much easier for the gardener) to adapt indigenous plants to the landscape than to plant what may not flourish in your region.

Evaluate your space and learn about the plants native to your area that might be incorporated into your Arts and Crafts garden. Think carefully about the flowers and accents that will successfully unite your house with the garden and begin planning how you will include these special accessories and plants. Keep in mind that planning and patience are essential when gardening. An instant garden never gives the satisfaction that unfolds with care and time.

4

DESIGN OF THE ARTS AND CRAFTS INTERIOR

PRECEDING PAGES: *An open floor plan, with furniture placed to promote conversation, centers family activity around the welcoming hearth. The main rooms of Arts and Crafts houses usually boast generous proportions, allowing family and visitors to gather comfortably.*

Superb interior construction and well-thought-out floor plans for their houses were critical to the architects of the Arts and Crafts Movement, who were striving to improve the character of a house's inhabitants as well as the quality of the building. By using local materials that were well suited to a particular climate, the designer ensured a house that would keep its family safe and warm in harsh weather and comfortably cool during sweltering summers. New ideas about open floor plans encouraged communication in the home, and modern conveniences made life just a bit easier for everyone. With a desire for beauty and a respect for utility, Arts and Crafts architects built houses that continue to serve their occupants well through the generations.

OPPOSITE: *Fine architectural details and gleaming woodwork are hallmarks of Arts and Crafts interiors. A built-in desk and bookcases harmonize with the mantelpiece in a seamless panel. The mass of wood is gently relieved by subtle color in the pottery, light fixtures, carpet, and flowers.*

LEFT: *Arts and Crafts architects encouraged the use of local materials and vernacular styles, and thus the woodlands of the Northeast were an appropriate setting for a log cabin. The deep tones of wood pair beautifully with mossy greens, ocean blues, dark golds, terra-cottas, and other earthy hues.*

REGIONAL MATERIALS

AN AUTHENTIC ARTS AND CRAFTS house is made from the natural resources of the region in which it is located—a house in the woods should be constructed of logs cut from the forest that surrounds it. Similarly, the interior finishings of true Arts and Crafts homes are determined by the particular resources at hand.

The trees common in different geographical areas supplied woods for the houses in the vicinity. Depending on the area in which the house was located and upon the budget of the owner, cedar, oak, fir, or mahogany might have been used. In the West, California bungalows proudly display redwood doors and paneling, and in the Southwest cypress wainscots are prevalent in houses near spots where these trees grew.

In the East, the American chestnut was a particularly valuable tree for the lumber industry because its great height meant more wood, and therefore more profit, per tree. However, an epidemic known as the chestnut blight, a result of the importation of Asian chestnuts in the 1890s, virtually killed off the American species of the tree. As a result of the chestnut blight, the lumber industry had a surplus of this beautiful, quality wood at lower prices for immediate use by Craftsman designers. Many eastern dining rooms of the period are paneled with this treasured chestnut. The epidemic itself served as a poetic reminder of the dangers of importing exotics, and its converse, the value of using indigenous materials .

Typical Arts and Crafts fireplaces and chimneys are made of stone, stucco, brick, or locally found rocks, and nearby potteries often provided tile for the fireplace surround. Local materials are always preferred for construction because they naturally suit the climate and therefore provide the most comfortable living conditions. The use of regional construction materials is both economical and representative of the Arts and Crafts ideal of working in rhythm with nature.

BELOW: *New construction in the Arts and Crafts style allows for updated interpretations of the philosophy. In this modern interior a wall of glass provides an inescapable link with nature. Traditional elements such as wooden beams and a fireplace of native stone place the design firmly in the Arts and Crafts mode.*

FLOOR PLANS

A MAJOR TENET of the Arts and Crafts Movement was the deliberate withdrawal from the formal etiquette and elaborate social rituals that dominated the Victorian era. The belief was that such pretense stifled clear communication and genuine intimacy. This new philosophy held that an individual is not separate from others or from nature, but rather that the world consists of interconnected persons, each with his or her individual gifts and personal expressive style.

The layout of Arts and Crafts houses reflects an intention to encourage family unity, endeavoring to create a feeling of intimacy and retreat from the stressful world outside. Open floor plans became the norm, as parlor doors were deemed unfriendly and old-fashioned.

An Arts and Crafts plan, whether large or small, always conveys a feeling of spaciousness, even if space is in fact limited. Because ceilings were lower than in decades past, an open floor plan and larger windows prevented the rooms from appearing dark and claustrophobic. Typically, more than one room is visible

ABOVE: *Frank Lloyd Wright sought to "break the box" in order to create new and exciting living spaces. The rooms in Victorian houses were traditionally squared off and well-defined by four walls and a door. Wright's open interior spaces were defined more by rugs, natural wood, and furniture groupings. Here a "room within a room" is created by lines of wood and carpet geometrics. Varying ceiling heights, as in the smaller dining nook shown here, are another method Wright used to make his living spaces more interesting.*

RIGHT: *In Arts and Crafts houses, the living room and dining area are typically open to each other. Here, a large squared arch fosters flow from one space into the other. Oriental screens had been popular during the Victorian era and continued to be used in Arts and Crafts houses to redefine space.*

from each part of the house. This is a far cry from the Victorian house, with its formal, individual rooms, each serving its own function and closed off from neighboring rooms by single or sliding double doors. To break up the openness, dividing half columns above solid panels, built-in bookcases, or china cabinets sometimes separated living and dining areas from hallways or other areas.

The stairway and railing of Arts and Crafts houses are usually exposed and visible from the living room or hallway. Often, ceiling beams and other construction features were left open to view, emphasizing the importance of structure. Logs and stone that appeared rough-hewn or handcut only underlined the sense of handcraftsmanship with which the house had been built.

Notably absent from most Arts and Crafts houses are the servants' quarters considered integral to grand Victorian homes. For the most part, Arts and Crafts houses, particularly bungalows, were conceived for citizens of the middle class, who often had a "day girl" but did not have the wherewithal to hire live-in help. Even in houses commissioned and built by the well-to-do the presence of servants was understated, in keeping with the Arts and Crafts ethic, which decried a life of luxury and elaborate social nonsense as unproductive and unhealthy.

KITCHENS

TWO INVENTIONS that were installed in virtually every home by the beginning of the twentieth century were electricity and indoor plumbing. While these conveniences were vast improvements over the gas or candle lighting and pumped water and outhouses of years previous, they pale in comparison to the options in time-saving appliances available today. Nearly one hundred years later, the kitchen is the room most likely to be enlarged in newly built or renovated Arts and Crafts houses.

A modern preference for large kitchens that include such luxuries as fireplaces and dining and sitting areas has led to what we now call "great rooms." Most Arts and Crafts kitchens are relatively small in size and may not have enough space to accommodate all the features now considered essential. Kitchens in Craftsman houses were planned with efficiency in mind. Economy of movement was key, and small kitchens meant fewer steps between refrigerator, sink, stove, and cabinets. Adding onto to the kitchen or annexing space from another room can expand the space in your period Arts and Crafts kitchen, creating a great room if that is what you desire.

LEFT: *This English country kitchen has recently been enlarged and renovated—the latest commercial-quality equipment was installed, paired with period-style cabinetry and antique furniture. The work table, designed by Edward Mouseman, is an excellent example of Arts and Crafts furniture from the Cotswolds. Note the light color of the walls, which was typical in kitchens of the era.*

BELOW: *An open, airy new kitchen captures the Arts and Crafts feeling with paneled wood cabinetry, beautifully crafted shelving, and a box beam ceiling. Reproduction twig chairs and an old oak desk pressed into service as a table add rustic appeal, while tribal rugs and a light fixture inspired by Arts and Crafts lamps complete the scene. This comfortable, attractive kitchen is a fine example of Craftsman styling mixed with modern proportions and state-of-the-art stainless steel appliances.*

If this is how you plan to proceed, make sure to consult a qualified contractor who is sympathetic to the unique character of your Arts and Crafts house.

You may decide to simply renovate in order to maximize the space you have. There are several viable approaches for kitchen renovations in existing bungalows. One approach is to create a decor loosely in the Arts and Crafts style; this plan produces a more glamorous result than originally existed in modest bungalows or log cabins while maintaining a look compatible with the rest of the house.

One of the latest trends in kitchen design is to furnish the room with stand-alone pieces in lieu of built-in cabinetry. Separate work stations for each activity can be placed throughout the kitchen—a mini wine cellar or cooler, a fireplace spit for cookery, preparation areas with separate sinks, and even an old-fashioned larder and pantry. Though built-in cabinets were typical, and were admired for their space-saving aspect, Hoosier cabinets—large, free-standing, all-purpose work stations—were also popular. If you have a small kitchen, you may not have space

LEFT: *Modern kitchen luxuries like a breakfast bar and a large center island are tempered with Arts and Crafts–era lanterns and Mission-style stools. A copper range hood, Craftsman-style hardware on the cabinets, and an art glass window in the back door are further links to the Arts and Crafts period. Weathered exposed beams and local stone give the room an age-old look.* BELOW: *If your kitchen has original fixtures or if you can find period pieces, it is well worth the cost to recondition them. Not only will refurbished appliances function beautifully, they can be appreciated as fine sculpture.*

to include all, or even most, of the kitchen furniture mentioned here, but just one or two pieces can add to the character of the room.

You may also be using the Arts and Crafts era for inspiration in decorating a kitchen in a house that is not Craftsman. Whether or not your kitchen itself is truly Arts and Crafts, there are several things you can do to re-create the feel of the style. The use of natural woods and decorative tile is common, and many designers have returned to the white, enameled look (now often achieved with easy-care plastics or Formica), finished with decorative, old-fashioned, hexagonal tiles. Other authentic colors to consider are dark green or medium gray with white trim and fixtures.

Certainly, an updated interpretation of the past is more desirable than a museum-like re-creation. Only a purist would give up a dishwasher, food processor, microwave, or freezer, none of which appeared in original Arts and Crafts kitchens. These appliances needn't be hidden, though some clever designers have managed to do that.

For a more affordable solution to kitchen renovation, consider refacing existing cabinets. The original shelf construction may be better than what is available in modestly priced cupboards on the market now. A good Arts and Crafts resource

ABOVE: *A modern kitchen features a wealth of Arts and Crafts charm. While all of the appliances and furnishings are new, they have been chosen in sympathy with the Arts and Crafts Movement. Tile in a muted shade of green features a geometric band that adds interest without being showy. Expanses of wood are punctuated with period-style hardware, while a copper pendant lamp with mica shade and select pottery pieces provide colorful and attractive accents.*

store or artisan (see the Resource Guide on page 151) can make beautiful door and drawer fronts with hand-hammered or cast-metal hardware.

There are also Arts and Crafts border papers and wallpapers suitable for kitchens; glazing and stenciling can be the perfect solution and will give you the opportunity to be an artisan in your own home.

Another final option is to detach completely from the Arts and Crafts style and create a more modern design that employs the most efficient kitchen technology available today. This plan gives you the most freedom to incorporate the features you want without concern for the style of the rest of the house, but it does have a few drawbacks. If you have a vintage Arts and Crafts kitchen, you may be getting rid of beautiful old pieces in service to a desire for the newest innovations. However, while this type of renovation pains collectors and many Arts and Crafts enthusiasts, it may be inconsequential to the cook who must use the kitchen. A sleek modern-style kitchen is most likely to work if your house is more eclectic in nature, with select Arts and Crafts pieces, rather than pure Craftsman.

BATHS

THE DECORATING ADMONITIONS that apply to the kitchen also hold true for the bath, which was a new luxury at the turn of the century. While the original owners of many Craftsman houses were satisfied with a small bathroom, today glorious bathrooms with sinks, toilets, and Jacuzzis, each occupying separate alcoves, have become more important to some builders and renovators than a home's total square footage, the number of rooms, or the inclusion of a garage.

Creative additions to existing Craftsman houses now incorporate master suites with his-and-her baths and private adjoining sitting rooms. Perhaps, even for Arts and Crafts enthusiasts, constant togetherness is too much of a good thing.

Arts and Crafts bathrooms usually featured rectangular white tiles on the bottom portions of the walls, with the small tiles on the floor in the familiar octagonal shape. For people living at the turn of the century, white denoted cleanliness; armed with a relatively recent knowledge of germs, they much admired wipe-clean surfaces. A mirrored medicine cabinet and built-in storage for linens was also common.

ABOVE: *A mirrored medicine chest framed in wood reflects an art glass window in this small period bathroom. Burnished brass hardware on the cabinet and suitably old-fashioned faucets complete the look. Simple yet elegant, the marble walls and sink surround recall the importance of sanitation in the Arts and Crafts scheme.*

LEFT: *This bath, like other Arts and Crafts–inspired room designs, takes its cue from nature. Stone blocks are bordered at the top with a redwood-stained ribbon of lumber. The walls, sponged white over the faintest blue, recall wisps of clouds in a summer sky. Set safely in the window niche is a stunning display of art pottery.*

As today, sink, tub, shower, and toilet were usual fixtures of "ultimate bungalows," with the toilet and washing facilities sometimes separated. If your bathroom lacks its original fixtures or replacements in an appropriate style, you can find appealing reproductions of pedestal sinks and fixtures with wooden accoutrements that are practical as well as nostalgic. Claw-foot tubs, once again available, add a comforting touch of the past. These giant raised tubs can be outdone only by a sauna, steam room, or whirlpool. Home water therapy (hot tubs, power showers, and so on) is sensual and comforting, and much needed with the stressful demands of life in the 1990s.

Lastly, don't discount the possibility of an ultramodern remodeling project. If it suits you and your lifestyle, it can be a wonderful solution. It may best enable you to follow the primary principle of the Arts and Crafts Movement: Take care of your family and yourself by creating a home that echoes your ideals.

$\widehat{}$ $\widehat{}$ $\widehat{}$

Every aspect of the Arts and Crafts interior was designed with the philosophies of the movement in mind, chief among these: Love your work and improve your quality of life by creating a nurturing environment and protecting those you love. Harmony with nature and focusing on the positive were considered keys to happiness in the Arts and Crafts era—and they are again today.

OPPOSITE: *An English Arts and Crafts bath includes freestanding furniture, period artwork, and antique fixtures, a look that could be duplicated with quality reproductions. The starkness of a true period bathroom has been allayed with gleaming tiles in a deep teal. Walls have been painted white but trim is a creamy ivory, a treatment that warms the room and provides a pleasing neutral backdrop for other accoutrements.*

LEFT: *A spectacular period effect can be achieved with white tile, dark colored walls, and Mackintosh-style fittings. The pristine furniture and fixtures combined with the geometric quality of the French door's panes and the mirror's decorative sidelights give this bath the clean beauty characteristic of Glasgow-style rooms.*

5

INTERIOR DETAILS OF THE ARTS AND CRAFTS HOUSE

PRECEDING PAGES: *Archi-*
tectural details can create a
truly breathtaking interior,
rendering the room a work
of art. In this Greene and
Greene–designed master bed-
room, a glass clerestory provides
lots of light as well as an inter-
esting visual element. The
French doors to the sleeping
porch, too, brighten this glam-
orous room. The art glass lamp
and Oriental carpets bring color
and harmony to the setting.

RIGHT: *A cloud lift theme is*
repeated in the frieze above the
fireplace, the lantern, furniture,
and glass cabinet doors of
Greene and Greene's Gamble
House living room, as well as
throughout the rest of the house.
The theme is subtly yet effectively
displayed, tying together various
parts of the house and different
elements of the interior.

Interior architectural details and the decoration of walls, floors, ceilings, and windows are particularly significant because of the open floor plans that characterize most Arts and Crafts houses. This type of open scheme demands a continuity of theme and consistency of color and design. The wall finishes, window treatments, and hardware need not be identical, but they must be harmonious. Dramatic contrasts and conflicting patterns are undesirable, as they are inconsistent with the spirit of unity that defined the Arts and Crafts Movement and continues to dominate the Arts and Crafts design style. The general rule is to stick with subtle variations on one theme.

THEMES

MOST ARCHITECT-DESIGNED houses of the Arts and Crafts era follow one inspirational theme, which effectively integrates the rooms and offers poetic repetition throughout the house. Often these themes were stylized flowers or other objects from nature, though geometric forms were also widely used.

CHARLES SUMNER GREENE AND HENRY MATHER GREENE

Like several other influential architects of the day, including Frank Lloyd Wright and Charles Rennie Mackintosh, the Greene brothers conceived their houses as integrated environments, and often designed not only the structure but also the lighting, furniture, and interior detailing as well.

American architects and designers Charles (1868–1957) and Henry (1870–1954) Greene studied at the Massachusetts Institute of Technology in Cambridge, Massachusetts, later setting up practice together in Pasadena, California. Known for designing "ultimate bungalows" for wealthy patrons, the brothers established workshops using the best artisans to execute their fabulous designs.

Greene and Greene viewed the house as a whole, and often designed furniture, light fixtures, and other pieces to complement their interior architectural spaces. The ebony pegs and superb joinery notable in their work prompted C.R. Ashbee to comment that theirs was the best craftsmanship he saw on his trips to America. A special blend of Arts and Crafts in the Prairie style with a strong Japanese influence made the pair extraordinarily successful. Unfortunately, their designs were soon widely copied at lower cost and inferior quality.

For the Gamble House, the celebrated architects Greene and Greene chose an Asian cloud lift motif. This design is repeated in major and minor details throughout the house, from focal points such as the main beam of the inglenook to the switch plate for the lights. The cloud lift theme is unmistakably present, yet understated, an effect that has been praised by Arts and Crafts expert Randall Makinson as "a symphony of harmony in design."

RIGHT: *Abstractions from na-*
ture were a central theme used
throughout most of Frank Lloyd
Wright's Prairie house designs.
An understated geometric motif,
appearing here in cabinet glass,
is carried through windows and
lanterns in other parts of the
house. In many of Wright's
houses, the chosen motif extends
to textile and tile expressions
as well.

Frank Lloyd Wright chose more earthy elements for his houses. For the Dana Thomas House in Springfield, Illinois, Wright chose the sumac plant for his unifying symbol. The Hollyhock House in Los Angeles, California, not surprisingly, bears the tall, yet humble hollyhock as both its name and motif.

FIREPLACES

THE FIREPLACE REPRESENTS THE HEART of the Arts and Crafts house. Home and hearth convey the comfort and communication that is the cornerstone of the Arts and Crafts philosophy. The large and impressive stone fireplaces found in lodges and camps are reminiscent of fires built out of doors

LEFT, TOP: *This simple but elegant fireplace displays beautiful wood joinery at the corners of the raised hearth. The overmantel, rendered in a delicate sage green, is almost a mirror image of the more robust brick fireplace beneath it. Brick and stone were favorite choices for Arts and Crafts fireplaces, with construction materials often reflecting the resources of nearby industries or quarries.*
LEFT, BOTTOM: *Tile was another popular material for fireplace surrounds. This mottled, rosy-hued tile is punctuated by tiny tiles set in a flowing pattern around the fireplace. The addition of a colorful art pottery collection, built-in cabinetry, sconces, and a complementary architect-designed firescreen completes this scheme.*

within a circle of stones. Gathering round such a fire recalls the promise of warmth, nourishment, and protection that campfires and hearths have offered since the dawn of civilization. The fireplace is an identifying mark of an Arts and Crafts house, and its presence in houses of this period illustrates the timeless idea that a house with a fireplace is truly a home.

Fireplaces are also effective focal points of a room for decorating purposes, and the smallest bungalow, even in a warm climate, benefits from a blaze on chilly nights and damp days. Mantels, whether the fireplace they rest over is large or small, offer premier display spots, with every eye instantly drawn there.

Arts and Crafts–era fireplaces were usually constructed of stone, river rocks, or brick, and were sometimes faced with subtly hued tile. Hand-hammered copper hoods, often bearing favorite mottoes, graced some Arts and Crafts fireplaces. The copper hoods were not only decorative, but enhanced heat reflection as well.

ABOVE: *Flanked by wooden pillars wrapped in sheets of copper, this clinker brick fireplace creates a cozy spot.* RIGHT: *A slip of patterned tile decorates a natural pine mantelpiece in this cozy room. Accents of highly polished English copper contribute a warm yet sophisticated look; the decorative fireplace shield is emblazoned with pine cones, a popular motif of the Arts and Crafts period. The rich ochre walls, Liberty-print drapes, and geometric rug in rust tones impart a golden glow to the space. Note the square piano in the corner, designed by architect M.H. Baillie Scott.*

LEFT: *Handsome, space-saving, and finished with all the care used in free-standing furniture, this sideboard is elegantly accented with leaded glass cabinet fronts. A stained glass window set above it garners the piece extra attention. Finely crafted built-in furniture is one of the hallmarks of an Arts and Crafts interior.*

BUILT-IN PIECES

BUILT-INS OF ALL KINDS are common architectural details of the Arts and Crafts house that distinguish its interior from all others. These furnishings combine beauty and utility, and are ingenious in the spare and open look favored by many Arts and Crafts designers. Seating areas, too, could be built in, providing a quiet corner for reading or sewing.

Inglenooks, semi-enclosed seating areas in front of the fireside, derived from medieval designs. Great halls of the Middle Ages were usually drafty and cold, and an arrangement of tall benches on either side of the fireplace created a warm and sheltered spot. The inglenook provided a place of intimacy and warmth near the fire, perfect for quiet chats, reading, or daydreaming. Bookcases and drawers were often part of the structural arrangement,

Window seats, like inglenooks, are spaces designed for reflection or intimate conversation, and bring the bonus of a view of the landscape, emphasizing again the link of the house with nature.

ABOVE: *A built-in bookcase topped with a short, squared column was often used to divide the area between the living and dining rooms. The built-in bookcases and china cabinets so prevalent in Craftsman houses make great display cases for collections of pottery and metalware as well as for books, glassware, and china.*

RIGHT, TOP: *This stunning rendition of a built-in sideboard with stained glass windows is as useful and beautiful today as it was at the turn of the century when the house was built. The colorful glass relieves an expanse of wood that might otherwise seem overbearing; the vine theme of the windows brings nature into the house.*

RIGHT, BOTTOM: *A set of drawers built into the entryway makes use of the lost space beneath the stairs. The darker wood of the drawers attracts attention to the feature and creates a pleasing contrast of wood tones. Perfect for storing gloves, scarves, and other accessories, this built-in chest is also an extremely practical addition to the entry hall.*

LEFT: *Paneled wainscoting to a plate rail was a popular dining room wall treatment in the Arts and Crafts era. The surface above the plate rail was usually painted in a warm hue or, in England especially, papered in a nature-inspired pattern. This house features a rare oil on plaster mural, entitled* Times of the Day, *painted by Roycrofter Alexis Fournier.*

INTERIOR
DETAILS
87

WALL TREATMENTS

BEAUTIFUL WOOD PANELING is commonly found in houses of the period, and in fact, careful craftsmanship of all the woodworking in the house is a hallmark of an Arts and Crafts interior. Walls in the dining room were often paneled up to a plate rail, with the wall above painted with a mural or with a deep solid color, or in some regions, stenciled or wallpapered. The dining room is also the most likely room to feature exposed ceiling beams, though these sometimes appeared in other rooms as well, particularly in rustic houses. Typical in the living room was wainscot paneling or a chair rail topped by a picture rail.

The area above the paneling is prime space for decoration. Fabric, wallpaper, or paintings make excellent finishing touches, and draw one's eye upward. The band of wall near the ceiling, known as the frieze, can be treated to a wallpaper border or to stenciling, an inexpensive touch that complements the rich wood of the paneling.

Wall colors in the more public spaces of most Arts and Crafts houses range from buff, tan, rose, and gold to rich greens, blues, and burgundies. The idea was to create a sense of welcome and well-being, enveloping visitors and family alike with deep, warm hues. Dense pigments are popular again after half a century of white and beige dominating the interiors of most houses. Recent investigations into

ABOVE: *A plaster frieze decorated with Oriental-style flowering branches offers a subtle contrast to exposed joinery in a serene balance of feminine and masculine expression.*

RIGHT: *A stenciled frieze is an elegant yet inexpensive wall treatment that can be used in place of wood detailing or wallpaper. The appliqué on the portiere (a hanging curtain used to separate rooms) complements but does not repeat the stencil, resulting in a more complex and interesting space.*

BELOW: *Stenciling rendered in earth tones divides the wall, creating a frieze, rail, and field. This simple yet pleasing scheme has been carried out according to William Morris' advice on wall treatments.*

OPPOSITE: *Inspired by the Scottish countryside, Mackintosh's signature color scheme includes black, white, and grays punctuated by pinks and purples representing the heaths and heathers that grow in that region. The color contrasts, patterns, and designs incorporating positive and negative spaces add interest to a simple entryway.*

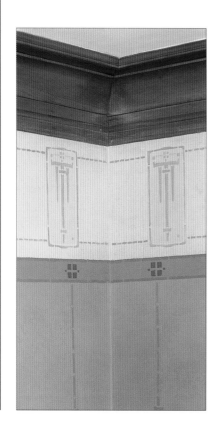

the importance of color reinforce the ideas of turn-of-the-century decorators, who proclaimed the healing properties of deep tones.

Some Arts and Crafts designers departed from these colors, however. Architect Charles Rennie Mackintosh used black, white, and gray with splashes of color, often pinks, purples, or cobalt. This scheme reflected the colors of Scotland in winter, with its snow-covered landscape dotted with bright heather.

Arts and Crafts bedrooms are generally done in lighter colors, with woodwork painted either white or a softer matching color. Presumably, the dainty lavenders, pinks, and yellows common in bedrooms were more in keeping with sweet dreams.

While wallpaper was not common in North America during the Arts and Crafts period, it was very popular in England, where William Morris made a name for himself with fabulous printed papers and fabrics. Stylized flowers with fruit, birds, and other animals were the most common themes for these papers, which bring nature into the house in true Arts and Crafts fashion. Today, several companies carry reproductions of Morris, C.F.A. Voysey, J. H. Dearle, and other Arts and Crafts designer fabrics and wallpapers. (See the Resource Guide on page 151.)

ABOVE: *Plain, sheer curtains filter light and partially screen windows in this elegant bungalow. The simplicity of Arts and Crafts houses is incompatible with fussy window treatments, and bare or minimally dressed windows are the ideal. In this treatment, even the curtain rods are invisible (hidden above the window casings), lending the panels a pure quality unmarred by the shirred tops of the curtains.*

WINDOW DRESSINGS

URTAINS AND OTHER WINDOW TREATMENTS are necessary for privacy in sleeping chambers. Sheer lace or opaque fabrics are appropriate and were commonly layered over shades for double protection, with heavier material over the sheers for greater insulation.

In living areas, curtains of homespun, stenciled or embroidered at the bottom, are the most memorable Arts and Crafts window treatments. Shirred on simple wood, brass, or wrought-iron rods, fabric curtains should be generous but not full. Excessive draperies are never the right solution in an Arts and Crafts house, and bare windows are often just right.

Other attractive window coverings include bamboo and matchstick blinds, which suited bedrooms, sleeping porches, and sunrooms. Venetian blinds became popular in Europe during the Arts and Crafts era, and eventually the style traveled to the United States. Today, miniblinds and other modern window shades, including pleated screens, are a perfect way to achieve minimal window covering while still providing an adjustable block from street, sun, and foul weather.

FLOOR TREATMENTS

BEAUTIFUL HARDWOOD FLOORS, accented with area rugs, were the traditional flooring in Arts and Crafts houses. There are several acceptable choices for rugs, and while different styles may be mixed throughout a house, they are rarely seen mixed together in the same room.

William Morris, C.F. Vosey, and Frank Lloyd Wright, among others, produced carpet designs in flat, stylized floral or geometric patterns that were either hand loomed or machine made. Reproductions of floor coverings designed by Morris and Wright are available, and newer patterns that approximate the style are relatively

BELOW: William Morris' famous Hammersmith carpet graces the hardwood floors of many English Arts and Crafts–style homes. As with his textile and wallpaper designs, Morris relied on stylized natural forms for his carpet patterns. High-quality reproductions of his firm's carpets, wallpaper, and fabrics are available today, and impart an aura of authenticity to period design schemes.

RIGHT: *This home is fully furnished with a wonderful collection of turn-of-the-century Indonesian, European, and Persian rugs. Modern hand-made carpets are available and provide first-rate floor coverings, but machine-made examples in softer tones are most affordable and provide a completely acceptable alternative.*

OPPOSITE: *A lavish English Tudor-style hallway with carved decoration becomes even more elegant when rich Oriental carpets are added. Warm wood tones and a comfortable chair welcome visitors into this gracious interior.*

easy to find. Depending on your budget, you can choose among high-priced replicas or less costly machine-made reproductions.

Oriental or tribal rugs and carpets—old or new, handmade, or machined—are just right for Arts and Crafts interiors. Hopi or Navajo designs match beautifully with rustic furnishings, and good-looking reproductions of these rugs are being made in Mexico. Collectors often favor authentic antique pieces but these are costly and rare.

A warm and welcoming interior, filled with beautiful wood built-ins and accented with subtle patterns in rugs and wallpaper, draws guests into the rhythm of the home. Cozy firesides and deep soothing colors complete the invitation, rendering the Arts and Crafts home a haven for all who enter.

6

FVRNITVRE

PRECEDING PAGES: *This inviting dining room is period perfect. Table and chairs, beautifully crafted in Mission oak style, are complemented by a Craftsman sideboard complete with copper hardware. Built-in china cupboard, cabinets, and drawers provide a fabulous backdrop for the free-standing furniture. Accents of art pottery, table runner, and carpet add color and visual appeal. A textured wall treatment in a warm apricot hue reinforces the room's charm.*
RIGHT: *This small Stickley table features an inlaid pattern on its top; typically, inlays were done with copper, pewter, and lighter- or darker-colored wood. The reproduction Old Hickory chair is a rustic design in wood and wicker; the appliquéd throw pillow completes this sunny scene.*
BELOW: *Legendary rush-seated maple chairs like this one served as the basis for the Mission chair. The originals were made by Forbes Manufacturing for San Francisco's Swedenborgian Church in 1895 to 1896. The design was copied, first by McHugh of New York City, and became a popular piece in Arts and Crafts homes.*

Nothing can enhance a home more than a beautiful piece of furniture. It not only advertises its owner's style, it symbolizes how he or she lives. The styles we choose define our homes, with cherished designs from the past imbuing the space with nostalgia and a pervading sense of comfort.

HALLMARKS OF ARTS AND CRAFTS FURNITURE

FURNITURE OF THE Arts and Crafts period has a distinctive character, though its appearance varies greatly depending on its region of origin, the particular sensibilities of its designer, and, in the case of commissioned furniture, on the tastes and needs of the client. But all Arts and Crafts furniture has this in common: whether a piece has sinuous Art Nouveau curves or stark Mission-style lines, the design is rooted in nature. All Arts and Crafts motifs are derived from plant, animal, human, or environmental forms.

Ideally, Arts and Crafts pieces are made, if not by hand, with much hand finishing. Unfortunately, handcrafted furniture was expensive and usually available only to wealthy clients. Some Arts and Crafts pieces were made with the general populace in mind, especially in America, where the use of machines was more accepted. In Arts and Crafts furniture, the very grain of the wood is counted as part of its decoration, and its sturdy construction is celebrated. Although the chief purpose of the hardware is functional, the fittings can have a handsome, honest, and appealing quality that adds to the piece's elegance.

BELOW: *Reproductions of an Old Hickory chair, wicker couch, and coffee table offer low-key furnishings for a casual room. An array of pillows decorated with the leafy designs and pine cones favored by Arts and Crafts proponents brings deep jewel tones to the setting. The drugget carpet and mica-shaded table lamp in the Limbert style are stylish period touches.*

RIGHT: *Well-designed furniture of solid construction was the aim of Arts and Crafts designers. This chunky oak table and chairs have a simple, solid quality that complements nearly any decor, and could be mixed and matched successfully with pieces of other eras. The heavy pieces are nicely softened by the glass-shaded chandelier and an assortment of fruit and flowers.*

In addition, the Arts and Crafts ideal promoted furniture that was both practical and beautiful, and that complemented the architecture of the house, so the home appeared as an organic whole. Arts and Crafts furniture design, like the architecture of the movement, was born of an intentional backlash against the overembellished designs and shoddy workmanship that resulted from the Industrial Revolution. The reverence for classical ornament and style was abandoned as Victorian ideals were rejected in favor of beauty inspired by nature and careful labor. The new aesthetic was expressed in different ways in various countries.

A B O V E : English and European Arts and Crafts furniture has more curves and decoration— all based on plant and animal forms—than American Mission furniture. William Morris advised that certain furniture, particularly nonessential pieces such as cabinets and side- boards, should be made "for beauty's sake" as much as for use, and that these pieces should be elegantly decorated with carving, inlaying, and painting.

GREAT BRITAIN

THE FIRST ARTS AND CRAFTS furniture designs were those created by Morris, Marshall, Faulkner & Co. in the 1860s. This company, often called simply "the Firm," pursued furniture designs that were beautiful in their simplicity, craftsmanship, and connection to tradition. They also produced pieces of more elaborate decoration, with handcrafted inlays of metal or mother-of-pearl or with decorative carving or paintings.

RIGHT: *Free-standing English kitchen furniture, like this large cupboard, was generally made of oak and adorned with hand-wrought iron or copper neo-medieval hardware. The Cotswold chair, out of the Gloucestershire workshops of Sidney Barnsley and Ernest Gimson, is more formal than the cottage cabinet, but the pairing works very well.*

ARTHUR HEYGATE MACKMURDO

British architect and designer A.H. Mackmurdo (1851–1942) studied the philosophies and designs of William Morris and John Ruskin, and went on to apply their ideas to the decorative furnishings he produced. Mackmurdo founded the Century Guild, which, though short-lived, was profoundly influential in the craft revival. Many of the pieces—including textiles, metalwork, and furniture—produced by the guild were designed by Mackmurdo.

Mackmurdo's furniture designs, some of which were described as proto–Art Nouveau, were much copied. The Mackmurdo foot, a bulbous base to the leg, on furniture was widely imitated by the Roycrofters and other Arts and Crafts cabinet and chair makers.

During the next three decades other craftguilds, such as A.H. Mackmurdo's Century Guild, C.R. Ashbee's Guild of Handicraft, and the more commercial Liberty and Co. followed, each with its own interpretation of the Arts and Crafts ideal.

At first, most of the designers continued to use turned Victorian spindles in their furniture; these can be seen on the original Sussex and Morris chairs. Sussex chairs were rush-seated and derived from traditional folk designs. These were manufactured for a wide distribution, rather than for the upper-middle-class patrons who commissioned many of the other Arts and Crafts pieces. The design for upholstered Morris chairs, with their distinctive adjustable backs, was designed by Philip Webb, who was inspired by a Sussex carpenter, and became a classic for Morris & Co.

Scotland's Charles Rennie Mackintosh was working on designs quite different from those in England. Early in the twentieth century Mackintosh and his wife, Margaret MacDonald, her sister Frances, and Frances' husband, Herbert MacNair, known as "The Four," devised a look that soon become known as "Glasgow Style"

ABOVE: *One of the most beautiful things about English oak is the warm honey patina it acquires with years of loving use. Note the wooden pegs used in place of nails.*

LEFT: *Except for the rose, the heart was the most popular Arts and Crafts motif on both sides of the Atlantic. This classy corner features a C.F.A. Voysey–style rush-seated chair with a heart-shaped cutout in its back. The pewter candle holder, designed by Archibald Knox, sits atop a leaded glass–fronted cabinet that also carries the heart motif.*

(sometimes referred to as the "Spook School"). Somewhat experimental in nature, the designs of the Glasgow School were criticized by English Arts and Crafts designers as allied with Art Nouveau, which they considered decadent.

Mackintosh and his collaborators designed total environments, matching the furniture to the architecture and complementing these with textiles, rugs, and other accessories that integrated the entire space. They created the stunning furnishings for Miss Cranston's tearooms—a commission that helped make Macintosh famous.

Macintosh's prize-winning designs for the Glasgow School of Art, in addition to the houses he created for well-known clients, brought him to the attention of the world. His fire burned brightly, but briefly, and he turned to an obscure career as a watercolorist.

RIGHT: *This room incorporates reproductions of Mackintosh furnishings, including his signature high-backed chair with geometrical cutouts, a simple black table, and a built-in cabinet. Textiles and stencils in muted colors feature the famed Glasgow rose. Together these elements present a sophisticated look that makes a strong statement.*

CHARLES RENNIE MACKINTOSH

White and black were Mackintosh's colors of choice for most of his furniture—it was his pallid color schemes and elongated forms that led his critics to designate the style as the "Spook School." The master bedroom of Hill House is a wonderful example of Mackintosh's work, which set the stage for the Vienna Secession and continues to inspire designers today.

ppreciation for the work of Scottish architect and designer Charles Rennie Mackintosh (1868–1928) has recently grown, and his designs are now valued for their elegant, flowing lines. Originally, Mackintosh's work was judged by many English proponents of Arts and Crafts as too close to Art Nouveau, which was felt to be somewhat vulgar.

Like many other Arts and Crafts architects, Mackintosh created integrated environments in which he (often in collaboration with his wife, Margaret MacDonald, her sister Frances, and Frances' husband Herbert MacNair) designed not only the building but also the furniture, textiles, wall treatments, and other elements.

Mackintosh's work was influential in Scotland and later in Europe, but after 1916 he worked on nothing but his watercolors of flowers, which today are praised for their wonderful quality. Mackintosh has been called the father of modern design.

ABOVE: *This bow-arm Morris chair first appeared in Gustav Stickley's 1902 catalog, and became a regular offering for the company. The slight bowing of the arms is echoed in the arched apron on the front and sides of the chair.*

RIGHT, TOP: *A matching, leather-covered foot stool was a common and practical accessory for Morris chairs. These adjustable reclining chairs were produced by every furniture maker in America and soon became synonymous with Arts and Crafts style.*

RIGHT, BOTTOM: *Gustav Stickley was known as the father of Arts and Crafts furniture in America, and his designs are widely reproduced today. This bedroom in Stickley's home, Craftsman Farms, features a lovely old oak bed with an inlaid headboard. The round table has legs that are flush with its top and half stretchers that are capped with a small finial, a simple but decorative touch. The oak furniture is softened with a comfortable wicker chair and homey accents like a table scarf, an art pottery vase filled with tulips, and Arts and Crafts–style bed linens.*

NORTH AMERICA

ONTRASTED WITH ENGLISH Arts and Crafts furniture, American Mission pieces seem rather severe, and indeed, the more basic, almost crude, designs foreshadowed the beginning of modern style. American Arts and Crafts designers aligned themselves with their early forebears, modeling their furniture on the simple but well-designed chairs, tables, and dressers of the pioneers. They were also influenced by the beauty and craftsmanship of Shaker furniture, which had been showcased at the Philadelphia Centennial Exhibition in 1876.

American entrepreneurs Gustav Stickley of Craftsman Workshops and Elbert Hubbard of Roycroft, unlike their British compatriots, embraced the machine as a means to make the new simple furniture. It is also likely that Frank Lloyd Wright's

ABOVE: *The architects Greene and Greene designed their furniture specifically for each commission. The Thorsen House in Berkeley, California, exemplifies their fascination with exotic woods, subtle curving lines, and exquisite joinery. These elements are also facets of the Japanese aesthetic, which the Greenes greatly admired.*

1898 lecture "The Art and Craft of the Machine" influenced their views. The new designs were intended to be relatively inexpensive and therefore to fulfill the mission of the Arts and Crafts Movement: to produce functional, substantial, and attractive furnishings for everyone.

Gustav Stickley, the best-known Arts and Crafts furniture maker in North America, helped set the trend with his Craftsman furniture line. Gustav had five brothers, and between them they had four separate companies, which created quite a bit of confusion. Most prominent was the Leopold and John George Stickley Co., which still flourishes today in a suburb of Syracuse, New York. The others were Quaint Furniture in Grand Rapids, Michigan, and the Stickley Chair Co. in Binghampton, New York.

In 1916, Gustav became partners with Leopold and John George following the bankruptcy of his own company. Although the liaison was short-lived, it gave L. & J.G.

BELOW: *This bedroom, designed for an elderly aunt, displays the softer side of Arts and Crafts. Feminine wicker paired with a brass bed is a lovely alternative in an Arts and Crafts room. A chaise and an armchair, together with a table and chairs, make up a small sitting area.*

GUSTAV STICKLEY

A pine cone appliquéd pillow, once featured in The Craftsman *magazine as a kit, adorns a Stickley-style chair. The pattern on cafe curtain and wallpaper was inspired by Roycroft china. While Stickley and Hubbard were chief competitors, their designs are highly compatible and are mixed together as often now as they were then.*

American designer and furniture maker Gustav Stickley (1857–1946) was born in Wisconsin and moved to Pennsylvania at the age of eighteen to learn chairmaking from an uncle. After a trip abroad he settled in Syracuse, New York, to found his furniture business. Stickley modeled his furniture after the simple pieces of the Shakers and of the early American settlers. After exhibiting in Grand Rapids in 1900 he enlarged his company and renamed it Craftsman Workshops.

From 1901 to 1916 Stickley published *The Craftsman*, a magazine that popularized his designs and those of his compatriots. He moved his enterprise to New York City in 1905 and founded Craftsman Farms, an ideal community farm. His overextended operation ultimately undid him, and the firm was taken over by L. & J.G. Stickley Co., which exists today making fine reproductions and reissues.

Stickley the rights to the designs of both enterprises. Today, the company is thriving and makes excellent reproductions of Arts and Crafts furniture, including eight pieces of licensed Roycroft reproductions. This situation must surely shake the ghosts of the two Arts and Crafts giants Gustav Stickley and Elbert Hubbard, who were once archcompetitors.

The straight slats and simple legs of Craftsman furniture were easily duplicated, and, consequently, there was an explosion of companies that began making Arts and Crafts–style furniture (this included Gustav's brothers). Sears, Roebuck and Co. was a leader in catalog sales of Arts and Crafts–style pieces, aggressively promoting its sturdy bedroom, dining, and living room Mission furniture suites.

Other influential American furniture designers were primarily architects who designed household furnishings to complement the interior spaces they had created. Greene and Greene and Frank Lloyd Wright fall within this league of designers, which owes much to the European Arts and Crafts tradition. Along with a handful of other architects and designers, Wright took the boxy-looking Arts and Crafts furniture designs and stretched them into elongated, elegant forms. And he used these forms in daring new ways, creating, for example, a "room" within a unique room with his signature high-backed dining chairs.

A B O V E : *Spindles, oak, and leather seats in Frank Lloyd Wright's famous dining rooms confirm the architect's identification with Arts and Crafts style.*
L E F T : *This fine drop-front has lots of cubbies for organizing writing accessories—its highly polished surface shows the lovely wood grain that Arts and Crafts designers considered part of the piece's decoration. The desk's placement beside a fabulous plate glass window is sure to offer inspiration to any writer.*

EUROPE

EUROPEANS, ESPECIALLY in Austria, France, Russia, Hungary, and Czechoslovakia, took a different artistic approach to the movement, as did a few Americans, including Louis Comfort Tiffany (working in glass) and Charles Rohlfs. Their Art Nouveau designs represented a different approach to art for the new century.

Beautiful, asymmetrical, curvaceous pieces based on the swirling designs found in nature echoed the lines of the Creator. Flowers, vines, clouds, shells, and even smoke inspired their lofty designs. The pieces were not inexpensive, but they were elegant. When they were copied by a machine, they seemed flimsy and garish by comparison.

Another European style drew from nature's inspiration, but with a manmade twist—or, more accurately, a lack of twist. These are the straight, stylized, and

ABOVE: While much of Austrian designer and architect Josef Hoffmann's early work was curvilinear, with typically Art Nouveau lines, his style evolved toward straight lines and minimal decoration, influenced by the designs of Charles Rennie Mackintosh. This sleek, Hoffmann-designed bedroom is both elegant and severe, the height of "the new style."

BELOW: *Eliel Saarinen, a Finnish architect who came to the United States in 1923, designed many houses in the Arts and Crafts style, known in Finland as National Romanticism. He was influenced by German and Viennese architects and designers, whose aesthetic is particularly evident in the squared cutouts of the long bench's arms. Leather-covered chairs with slightly scrolled arms are massive enough to hold their own in the large space.*

JOSEF HOFFMANN AND KOLOMAN MOSER

osef Hoffmann (1870–1956) and Koloman Moser (1868–1918), premier Austrian architects and designers, were much influenced by the work of C.R. Mackintosh, as well as by English Arts and Crafts designers such as William Morris and C.R. Ashbee. They asserted simplicity of line and decoration in their furniture, metalwork, and glass.

Hoffmann and Moser were both teachers and members of the Vienna Secession, the Austrian Art Nouveau Movement, which Moser founded. Hoffmann and Moser were known especially for exquisite metalwork, with Moser producing some very unusual lighting fixtures which on occasion included wooden beading and iridescent glass globe shades. Pieces were often marked WW for Wiener Werkstätte, a craft workshop the two founded in Vienna with Fritz Warndorfer as benefactor and commercial manager.

squared creations of the Vienna Secession. Josef Hoffmann and Koloman Moser, key figures in the Vienna Secession movement and later the Wiener Werkstätte (Vienna Workshops), were design reformers who found inspiration in the work of Scotland's Charles Rennie Mackintosh. They embraced a simpler, more refined aesthetic; while furniture was a mainstay of the Wiener Werkstätte, it grew to include almost every aspect of life, including fashion and jewelry.

In the past quarter century, enthusiasts have spent much time, energy, and money reviving interest in celebrated furniture designers such as William Morris, Charles Rennie Mackintosh, and Gustav Stickley. Great attention has been given to Elbert Hubbard's Roycroft, and there has been equal recognition of the magnificent work of the Greene brothers. Without question, the most successful of these revivals has been that of Frank Lloyd Wright, who has enjoyed accolades and near hero worship.

With this new-found appreciation of Arts and Crafts furniture design, myriad companies have begun making good reproductions, while galleries and auction houses have gathered collections of originals for sale. As an ideal marriage of art with craft, furniture brings a distinctive Arts and Crafts feeling to an interior, no matter the architecture of the house.

TOP: *This set of four bentwood chairs designed by Josef Hoffmann are richly upholstered and suitable for a formal dining room.* ABOVE: *The "Sitzmaschine," designed by Josef Hoffmann in 1905 and produced until 1938, was modeled after Philip Webb's reclining Morris chair. Considered a classic of Viennese design, the chair combines traditional bent beechwood with laminated wood in black.*

CHAPTER

7

LIGHTING

PRECEDING PAGES: *An intricately designed and colorful hanging lamp is the perfect complement to the solid Mission oak furniture and massive stone fireplace. Natural themes, like the grapes shown here, were as popular for lamp shades as they were for other Arts and Crafts furnishings and accessories.*
RIGHT: *Glass designer Dard Hunter's delicately arched tulip window lets an abundance of light into the Roycroft Inn's reception room. Allowing natural light to stream through undressed windows is the perfect way to light Arts and Crafts rooms during the day. The colors of the stained glass are repeated in the Viennese-style cylindrical sconce and the slag glass shade of the table lamp.*

✦━❈◈❈━✦

ABOVE: *A Dirk Van Erp milk can table lamp is resplendent with hand-hammered copper and the warm glow of mica. Widely reproduced, this wonderful form complements any Arts and Crafts setting.*

✦━❈◈❈━✦

Arts and Crafts lamps, now valued for their magical glow, were created with the intention of softening harsh electric lights in the turn-of-the-century home. Gas and kerosene lamps, which—along with sunlight, candlelight, and firelight—had been the chief method of lighting the home, were far more subtle when contrasted with the electric light bulb. To tone down the glare, Arts and Crafts designers turned to an array of materials to shade the bulbs, creating works of beauty out of pure necessity.

MATERIALS
AND DESIGN

BY COVERING INCANDESCENT BULBS with stained glass, mica, or colored blown glass, craftsmen created lovely shades of green, gold, and other delicate colors. Many lamp shades were made of mica, a transparent or subtly colored mineral that is found in thin layers. Shards of mica layered with shellac were usually bound together in a frame of copper, which gave the shade its shape. In tones of palest ivory through amber, these decorative shades softly filtered electric light, casting a golden glow over the room.

Stained glass was another favorite option for shading lamps, and designs ranged from simple geometrics to the elaborate Art Nouveau styles produced by Louis Comfort Tiffany and other glass designers working in his Tiffany Studios. Many architect-designers, such as Frank Lloyd Wright, Greene and Greene, and Charles Rennie Mackintosh, also designed lighting fixtures as part of their whole-design philosophy. Amber blown glass and frosted or pleated glass, in addition to linen, silk, or heavy parchment, were all used to create flattering lighting in the Arts and Crafts home.

The bases of Arts and Crafts lamps can be as artistic as the shades, and a variety of lamp bases can constitute a separate Arts and Crafts collection, the diversity of which adds to the subtle excitement of a sophisticated, yet informal, atmosphere. Many different materials were used to make the bases for Arts and Crafts table lighting, including quartersawn oak, walnut, or mahogany, art pottery, copper, wrought iron, bronze and leaded glass. Both reproductions and modern pieces inspired by the Arts and Crafts Movement have incorporated these various materials.

ABOVE: *This Handel Co. lamp is as precious as one of Tiffany's. These lamps were advertised in Roycroft's magazine and are much sought after by collectors today. The handsome heft of its bronze base and the muted chipped glass shade are a fine complement to the sturdy Morris chair.*

LEFT: *Louis Comfort Tiffany's well-known glass shades add color and pattern to an Arts and Crafts interior. This exquisite lamp features a base of water lilies and reeds growing up the column; the shade continues the theme with soothing greens and blues interrupted by buttery yellow flowers. Take care to match the style of the lamps to the character of the room; refined floral designs are most appropriate to rooms with an Art Nouveau or eclectic flair, while simple geometric lamps complement rustic log furniture and Navajo rugs.*

RIGHT: *Medieval-style lighting and accessories lend an Arts and Crafts room an authentic character and tie interior decoration to the original philosophies of the movement. A heavy iron chandelier filled with candles is a dramatic way to light a room; the fixture could also be converted to electricity, creating handsome and accessible lighting.*

ABOVE: *This table lamp, of leaded glass and hammered copper, was produced by the Roycrofters. One of their most successful designs, this graceful lamp works well in any Arts and Crafts setting.*

LIGHTING
THE ROOM

LANTERNS, FLOOR AND TABLE LAMPS, sconces, and chandeliers, all previously fueled with gas or kerosene, were redesigned to accommodate electric bulbs. The results were clean-looking, brighter rooms, with jeweled points of color and illumination that created an aura of comfort.

A variety of lighting fixtures in the room helps to avoid decorative monotony, though matching sconces and chandeliers in a dining room can create an inviting and harmonious look. A living area with several different kinds of shade treatments provides the most visual interest. It is also essential to site lighting fixtures at different heights; include hanging lamps, wall sconces, and floor and table lamps with bases of different lengths. Place accent lamps on furniture with surfaces of varying heights, such as end tables, console tables, desks, and mantels.

An odd number of fixtures is generally more pleasing than an even number, perhaps because the lack of pairing allows each lamp to be viewed as an individual thing of beauty rather than as one half of a deliberately matched set. Be sure to avoid making the lamps too evenly spaced or too close together.

Warm, flattering light is essential to Arts and Crafts style, but it need not be achieved with lamps alone. Gallery lights on oil paintings are an excellent way to provide subtle perimeter lighting. Natural light is a proven mood enhancer, and can provide most of your lighting during the day, particularly if you adhere to Arts and Crafts dictates on minimal window treatments. When the hour grows later, or if your house is shaded by trees, you'll need to supplement the waning natural light. Wherever possible, use dimmer switches to adjust the lighting to the mood or to the time of day.

BELOW: *These hanging lanterns of glass and copper are typical light fixtures in Stickley's Craftsman houses. A matching pair ensures that there is adequate lighting, while uncovered French doors let natural light into the room.*

For reading and other activities that require brighter light, high-tech halogen floor or table lighting can be used without ruining the look of the Arts and Crafts room. Many designs of the 1990s are compatible with turn-of-the-century pieces, yet provide functional task lighting. If you are buying a halogen or other high-intensity lamp for your home, look for a sleek, streamlined style in brass, brushed steel, or black, which is certain to blend well in your Arts and Crafts home.

Two Arts and Crafts Revival accessories that enhance the Craftsman appearance of a room are hand-hammered copper switch plates and outlet covers. Single, double, and triple covers that repeat the lighting fixture motif add architectural substance, especially to a modern room that lacks handcrafted wooden moldings and other details.

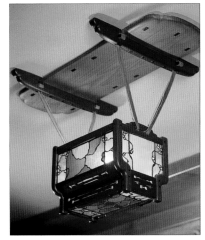

OPPOSITE: *Hanging fixtures like these Stickley lanterns, used in groupings or singly, were a very popular choice in the Arts and Crafts era. Matching sconces create a harmony between lighting elements and add valuable perimeter lighting in this peaceful dining room. The traditional table setting is illuminated by soft candlelight, another appropriate choice for evening.*

ABOVE: *This Greene and Greene lantern of wood and stained glass in amber, caramel, gold, and green is suspended on a pulley system over a dinner table. The design reflects the Japanese influence so prominent in the Greenes' work.*

LEFT: *Simple Arts and Crafts–style wall sconces of metal and glass provide ambient or task lighting in the kitchen, bath, or hall, and are available from a variety of sources.*

RIGHT: *This vertical Prairie-style table lamp is a fine match for the slim Arts and Crafts bedstead. Incorporated into the design of the lamp is a small pedestal for displaying pottery or other decorative items. The wash of light on the golden wall creates a gentle glow perfect for relaxing in bed.*

ABOVE: *Original Teco lamp bases and vases, which date from about 1904, were inspired by the architecture of the Chicago area. This lamp, with leaded glass shade and ceramic base, is a kerosene fixture and was intended for use in rustic camps, lodges, or log cabins, where electricity was not yet available. An electric version designed for a city setting was also available.*

FINDING
APPROPRIATE
LIGHTING

ONLY MUSEUMS AND A FEW WEALTHY collectors can afford signed, original Arts and Crafts lamps and light fixtures, but high-quality, reproduction lighting of every variety is available if you are willing to pay the price for fine craftsmanship (see the Resource Guide on page 151). Lamps and fixtures of lesser quality and poor design have also come to the marketplace, but they usually lack the subtle beauty of good lighting. If you are working with a limited budget, our suggestion is to buy one of the more expensive high-quality lamps, and gradually add to your collection as your budget permits. A few companies make sturdy, reasonably priced lanterns with opaque or slag glass that are quite suitable for kitchens, bathrooms, back halls, and stairways.

If you cannot afford high-quality original or good reproduction fixtures, you may be lucky enough to find an inexpensive antique base at a garage sale, flea market, or from an Arts and Crafts dealer. These are bargains only if you can find a competent artisan to design or build a suitable shade; this is likewise true for broken or damaged pieces. Always have lamps rewired for safety, and be sure to ask for silk cord (plastic will look awkward and should be avoided unless it can be completely hidden).

Poorly chosen lighting can ruin the look of an otherwise beautiful Arts and Crafts home. Select your pieces with care, using the best-quality reproductions you can afford and building your lamp collection little by little. Remember that a room bathed in soft light, with small pools of brighter light for reading or working, is your ultimate goal.

ABOVE: The ancient lantern shape was brought back into service during the Arts and Crafts era. Newly fitted with electricity, it proved as functional as it was decorative. Arts and Crafts designers also updated lanterns by adding ornamental cutouts, usually with natural or geometric motifs—the result was a piece that combined nostalgic appeal with state of the art technology.
LEFT: Frank Lloyd Wright first devised the indirect alcove lighting so popular in modern construction. These built-in lighting fixtures, composed of globes suspended within wooden frames, create a bright band above intricate geometric art glass windows.

POTTERY,
TILES,
AND GLASS

PRECEDING PAGES: *A mix of period Arts and Crafts pots and modern art pottery in green, mustard, and deep brown grace a reissued Stickley Mission oak sideboard. A bowl of ripe apples is a pleasingly natural accent; the bold print, massive hardware, and a new copper and mica lamp finish this strong statement.*

RIGHT: *This fine collection of rare Elton pottery is displayed in a period sideboard. Sir Edmund Elton, who established his Sunflower Pottery on his family's estate in England, experimented with a variety of metallic glazes. The crackled finish Elton used on some of his vases and jugs was achieved by firing them with layers of liquid gold and platinum.*

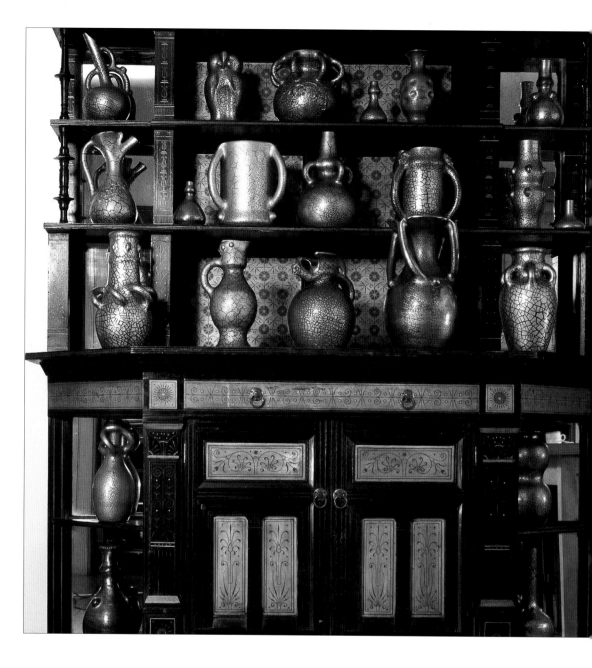

With some exceptions, Arts and Crafts pottery forms have their roots in the designs of ancient history, but what makes them unique is the influence of nature on their decorations and glazes. The prevalent matte green finish echoes plant leaves, and the flowers, frogs, and dragonflies with which much pottery is decorated reminds us of our connection to other living things.

More than perhaps any other medium, pottery popularized the Arts and Crafts style. The pieces were beautiful and, with some exceptions, affordable to average citizens. While many pots were hand-thrown, others were made from molds, allowing enough to be manufactured that quality pieces can be affordable even today.

The sparks of natural color that pottery introduces in a room provide a welcome contrast to the heaviness of oak and other woods. A special piece of pottery, like a painting, benefits from a location in which it is the focus of attention. Silk and dried flowers are acceptable for display in art pottery, but fresh flowers fully enhance the beauty of pottery pieces, and add life to their surroundings.

THE ENGLISH HERITAGE

POTTERY HAD A LONG and storied tradition in England, and potters of the Arts and Crafts era drew on this heritage, hearkening back to the methods, glazes, and designs of times past.

Renowned English potter William De Morgan worked first with Morris & Co., and then started his own pottery. His pieces, in shades of yellow, pink, silver, and gold had a marvelous iridescent quality. Flowers, fish, and other natural motifs were stylized to capture the spirit of their beauty. Later in his career, De Morgan turned to deep blues, reds, violets, and greens, often collaborating on pieces with his former employer and old friend William Morris.

Another notable British pottery was Della Robbia, which produced unique pieces and lovely ware for a relatively short span of time, only twelve years, before going out of business. Using the standard techniques for majolica, Della Robbia created vases, plates, jars, and other pieces decorated in colors of bluish green, yellow, orange, red, cream, and black. Most of us are familiar with the assortment of fruit and nut designs that inevitably make an appearance at holiday time.

Other potteries of note working in the Arts and Crafts vein include Doulton & Co., Josiah Wedgwood & Co., Pilkington's Tile & Co., William A. Moorcroft, and Ruskin Pottery. These and other smaller potteries produced a variety of wares in a myriad of colors, glazes, and forms, all owing their inspiration to nature and to the philosophy that encouraged beauty in design.

WOMEN IN ART POTTERY

IN ART POTTERY WOMEN finally had an outlet for creative expression other than sewing, embroidery, and other textile crafts that were considered household skills and rarely brought a good wage. Because decorating pottery seemed almost an extension of china painting, which had long been a popular ladies' pastime, women were quickly accepted.

In England, some potteries routinely employed women to decorate their wares. Doulton & Co., for instance, sold the pieces of Hannah Barlow and her sister Florence, as well as those of Eliza Simmance.

A few women founded potteries of their own, notably Maria Longworth Nichols, who started the Rookwood pottery in Cincinnati, Ohio. Rookwood pottery

ABOVE: *English Della Robbia pottery, produced for only a short time, is quite rare and offers unusual shapes and rich colors.*

ABOVE: *These exquisite vases share a subtle palette of blues and greens as well as motifs derived from nature. Several leading potteries, including Newcomb in New Orleans and Rookwood in Cincinnati, were founded for the purpose of providing women with a means for economic independence and creative expression. The pieces shown here were produced by Newcomb, left and center, and Rookwood, right.*

initially enlisted the help of men to throw and fire the pots, while women did the decoration; later, women did all of these tasks. The tonalist images on some Rookwood pots have a fantastic dreamlike quality and are much sought after by collectors.

Mary Louise McLaughlin, who had exhibited her painted china at the Philadelphia Centennial Exhibition in 1876, turned to pottery and proved one of the most experimental amateur art potters. She revolutionized glaze technology, experimenting with limoges-style hard-paste porcelains and various types of glazes at a kiln in her backyard.

Prize-winning potter Adelaide Alsop Robineau, who had studied art with Impressionist painter William Merritt Chase, handcrafted exquisite pieces in Syracuse. Robineau made some of the most elaborate hand-carved decorative pottery pieces in recent history. Robineau also published *Keramic Studio,* an influential magazine devoted to art pottery.

In addition to individual women who looked to pottery as a means of artistic expression and a way of earning money, several schools were founded for the express purpose of teaching women handcrafts as fine art and thereby enabling them to support themselves with their skills. Newcomb College at Tulane University in New Orleans was one such institution. Newcomb pottery's characteristic depictions of southern flora and fauna and its distinctive blue glazes make it among the most revered pieces in contemporary collections.

RIGHT: *Green pots in a matte finish were the top choice for Arts and Crafts pottery. Whether the pottery was produced by Teco, like the piece shown here, Grueby, or Weller, the natural green tones provided a harmonious link to quartersawn oak, copper accents, and golden art glass. Other pottery colors—gold, blue, and rose—existed but were used only moderately.*

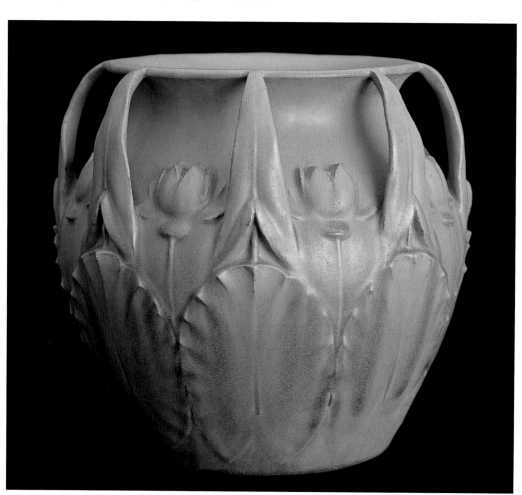

ADELAIDE ALSOP ROBINEAU

Connecticut-born Adelaide Alsop Robineau (1865–1929) learned watercolor and china painting, which she soon exhibited and taught. After marrying Frenchman Samuel Robineau, she edited a magazine called *Keramic Studio*, which had the mission of teaching good design in pottery.

Robineau's experiments in 1903 with porcelain and crystalline glazes promoted traditional designs. She worked with the celebrated French potter Taxile Doat until 1911 when she won the Grand Prix in the Turin International Exhibition for her famed scarab vase. Her glazes and high-fired porcelain work are beautifully sophisticated.

THE ART POTTERY
TRADITION CONTINUES

ART POTTERY WAS more prevalent in North America than anywhere else. The work of innovative American artisans was presented in exhibitions—such as the Philadelphia Centennial in 1876 and the Pan-American Exposition in 1901—that demonstrated the medium's unique ability to fully express the ideals of the Arts and Crafts Movement.

Pottery mass produced in molds did not, in general, suffer from low quality and poor design. Designers such as Frank Lloyd Wright, unlike their British counterparts, embraced the machine, accepting it as a fact of an industrial society and harnessing it to suit their purposes. Many mass-produced pots were in fact deemed as desirable as hand-thrown ones, and the designs of Teco are now among the most valuable. Teco—a line of the Gates Potteries named after Terra Cotta, Illinois, the town in which the pottery was located—was celebrated for its interesting, architectural forms. These "architectonic" shapes, designed by Frank Lloyd Wright, Louis Sullivan, and other well-known designers, are impressive miniatures of modern-style buildings. A matte green glaze is traditionally associated with Teco pottery, although mustard gold was also used.

In Boston, William Grueby began a pottery called the Grueby Faience Company that produced very popular pieces currently in great demand. The most sought-after Grueby pieces can be identified by their matte green finish, though the pots also came in shades of yellow, blue, brown, and purple. These lovely, subtle pieces were hand-thrown and typically decorated with flowers and foliage designs.

Much of the credit for the progress of art pottery in America goes to Alfred University in western New York and to the founding head of the ceramics department,

Alfred Binns, whose students have made history with their work. One of them, Frederick Walrath, deserves to be recognized for his richly colored pottery, usually subtly decorated with stylized flowers and foliage.

No discussion of Arts and Crafts–era pottery would be complete without a mention of Artus Van Briggle and George Ohr. Known as the "mad potter of Biloxi, Mississippi," Ohr became renowned for his oddly formed earthenware vessels, some of which featured wrinkles and folds about the neck and handles. He pushed the envelope in the pottery industry by crafting paper-thin vessels that he then allowed to collapse. The result is fascinating and rather bizarre. Van Briggle, who had been trained by Rookwood proprietor Maria Longworth Nichols, specialized in pieces with a distinct Art Nouveau look that incorporated human and floral designs.

Marblehead, Fulper, and Arequipa are among the other highly collectible Arts and Crafts potteries that integrate beautiful proportions, subtle colors, and matte finishes or glazes.

Many potteries of the early twentieth century imitated the avant-garde potteries in the industry. Peters & Reed, McCoy, Weller, and Roseville all made handsome designs in large quantities, often with the desirable matte green finish. These pieces are not found everywhere, but once located they are affordable and, displayed in groups of three, five, or more, look stunning on mantels, windowsills, bookcases, and benches. Roseville's Mostique pattern is a 1916 chunky style that features a rough, matte gray background with square yellow roses: this example epitomizes the Arts and Crafts generic pot in that it is attractive, affordable, and gorgeous when displayed.

ABOVE: *These vases, with their tactile matte glazes in blue, green, and violet, are by the Roycroft Renaissance master artisan Janice McDuffie. Already highly collectible, these hand thrown-pots reward their owners with as much satisfaction as vintage art pottery.*

ART POTTERY
TODAY

ART POTTERY PRODUCED IN the 1980s and 1990s is entirely acceptable in a house decorated in the Arts and Crafts style. No modern-day Arts and Crafts pottery is more desirable or beautiful than the pieces made by the Roycroft potters. Janice McDuffie is a master artisan working in the only craft produced on the Roycroft campus today. Her hand-thrown pots are collectible, and her green glazes and applied designs are worthy of comparison to most of the finest originals. No pots from the short-lived historic pottery at Roycroft have surfaced, although old advertising noted them as lovely.

Several other modern potters are creating superb vessels. The Nichibei Pottery in California produces a handsome molded green ware that is quite affordable. Jerome Venneman of California hand carves his molded pots and finishes them in three earthy glazes. Any of his designs make a stunning addition to an Arts and Crafts interior.

LEFT: *Art tiles were a signifi-*
cant building material indoors
and out, particulary in warmer
climates, where the tile was not
likely to be damaged by repeat-
ed freezes and thaws. Garden
walls were often decorated with
tile made by local potteries, and
sometimes incorporated foun-
tains as a special focal point.
This fountain, wreathed with
ivy, is faced with plain
unglazed terra-cotta tiles ac-
cented with tiles decorated with
molded figures.

TILES

MANY POTTERY COMPANIES also made tiles, and each region seemed to give rise to a local tileworks. Tiles were used to accent architecture, both interior and exterior, and some designers even incorporated tiles into their furniture. Gustav Stickley, in fact, used Grueby tiles in several of his small tables, and this pairing was introduced as a "furniture marriage" at the 1901 Pan-American Exhibition in Buffalo, New York.

Doylestown, Pennsylvania, was the home of Henry Mercer, maker of unique tiles, whose Moravian Pottery and Tile Works is once again active and making accurate reproductions of Mercer's original work. Mercer, an extreme romantic and eccentric, created tiles with designs that borrowed motifs from the local Pennsylvania

RIGHT: *Tiles can be combined in a striking interplay of sizes, textures, colors, and glazes, and can decorate areas as diverse as fireplace surrounds, wainscots, walls, floors, baths, paths, and pools. Tile is practical, beautiful, and easy to care for, and local sources can nearly always be found to provide stunning decorative tiles at a reasonable cost.*

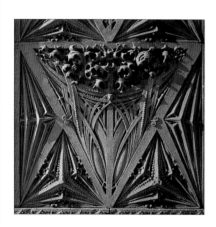

ABOVE: *Unglazed terra-cotta tile was used by turn-of-the-century architect Louis Sullivan for the exteriors of the Wainwright Building in St. Louis, the Auditorium Building in Chicago, and the Guaranty Building in Buffalo (detail shown here). Sullivan's architectural details were often richly ornamented with the curving lines distinctive to Art Nouveau.*

Dutch and from medieval castles throughout England. He called his home Fonthill, and this magnificent concrete and tile castle is now open as a museum house.

Detroit, Michigan, not only headquartered the burgeoning automobile industry, but also hosted the Pewabic Pottery company. Its tiles, which featured mythical creatures, graced many public buildings in the East and Midwest. Pewabic, too, is currently reproducing its designs at very affordable prices.

On the West Coast, no name is more recognized than that of Ernest Batchelder, who set up a craft school in Pasadena, California. Inspired in part by Ashbee's Guild of Handicraft and by the medieval designs that were the source for many artisans working in Arts and Crafts, Batchelder produced tiles and some pottery with stylized animals, flowers, and foliage. He also incorporated into his work Native American designs, Japanese-influenced motifs, and plants native to the West Coast. Replicas of Batchelder tiles are being made by Marie Tapp's Seattle restoration firm, which has been repairing original Arts and Crafts tiles for several years.

Reproductions of art tiles can be incorporated into restoration projects or additions to Arts and Crafts homes in various ways. A single tile displayed on a wall or set atop a table in a stand can be striking, while they also make practical and decorative coasters. A series of tiles can be used as a wall border or can be interspersed with common tile in a kitchen or bathroom. Historically, tiles were used to surround fireplaces, to cover hall floors, and as wainscot on entry walls. They add color and charm and are considered an integral part of the Arts and Crafts interior design.

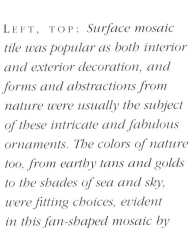

LEFT, TOP: *Surface mosaic tile was popular as both interior and exterior decoration, and forms and abstractions from nature were usually the subject of these intricate and fabulous ornaments. The colors of nature too, from earthy tans and golds to the shades of sea and sky, were fitting choices, evident in this fan-shaped mosaic by Louis Sullivan.*

LEFT, BOTTOM: *The cast terra-cotta frieze on this mantelpiece features rabbits, birds, and fruits in a hunting motif. Themes such as hunting and harvest were popular subjects for dining rooms, as well as for lodges or rustic camps. A functional surround of terra-cotta tiles frames the fireplace.*

BLOWN GLASS

As WITH OTHER SEGMENTS of the Arts and Crafts world, designs in glass emphasized an affinity for nature and an appreciation for "moral" forms. Thus, cut glass was abhorred because it was inherently unnatural, and therefore dishonest. Processes for producing pressed glass in molds were developed early in the nineteenth century, and this mass-produced glass was also deplored. Blown glass, with its more transparent, rounder forms was viewed by William Morris and his followers as more organic, and therefore closer to the Arts and Crafts ideal.

Perhaps the most famed glass designer of the era was Louis Comfort Tiffany, who together with Candace Wheeler founded the L.C. Tiffany Company and Associated Artists in 1879. The design talents of these two artists were manifested in many types of decorative items, but the lovely opalescent glass vases, perfume bottles, candy dishes, candlesticks, and plates are absolute treasures. These were made of an iridescent glass called Favrile, which was patented by Tiffany and featured at Bing's La Maison de l'Art Nouveau in Paris.

The Steuben glassworks in Corning, New York, also had a group of talented artisans. This company created "Aurene"—a vivid, opaque, colored glass—that was

LOUIS COMFORT TIFFANY

Son of the founder of Tiffany & Co., a firm specializing in silver, Louis Comfort Tiffany (1848–1933) first studied fine art and traveled abroad. With Candace Wheeler, a textile designer, Tiffany established Louis C. Tiffany and Associated Artists, which became an enormously successful decorating firm, with commissions that included the White House.

By 1885, however, he broke away and started the Tiffany Glass Co. He developed a process for "Favrile" glass, an iridescent glass that became exceedingly popular. Leaded glass lamps using bases of Grueby pottery were another specialty, and by 1900 the company had begun producing metalwork for lamp bases and other accessories. Tiffany left the business in 1919 although it continued until 1938.

transformed into decorative and functional items. Several Arts and Crafts lighting designers, including the Handel Co. and the Roycrofters, used lampshades of Steuben glass. Lalique in France and Dorflinger in Pennsylvania made clear, frosted, colored, and silver-decorated glass pieces, all of which are highly scouted by collectors.

Modern glass blowers have tried to duplicate the fabulous colors and sheer, sensuous texture of these great masters. None has succeeded because the original formulas were, for the most part, destroyed, but several attempts have come close. Lundberg glass from California could fool the eye of all but an experienced collector.

STAINED GLASS

STAINED GLASS WINDOWS in the Arts and Crafts style were first made by Morris & Co. following the dictates of Morris, who detested the overembellished Victorian stained glass, finding it out of character with the purity of his subjects, which were primarily biblical or mythical. The firm produced hundreds of stained glass pieces over its history, using the favored Arts and Crafts method of allowing one artisan to design and supervise all aspects of the project. This was in opposition to the typically Victorian practice, which relied on an assembly line to quickly produce a quantity of goods.

Louis Comfort Tiffany made fabulous art glass windows for churches and public buildings as well as leaded glass lampshades. Tiffany lamps skyrocketed in price in the 1970s and 1980s, and the name has come to refer to all leaded-shade lamps.

Other companies and artisians, too, took advantage of the big business in stained glass. Harry Clarke of Ireland produced fanciful windows in a saturated blue

ABOVE: *Charles Rennie Mackintosh's stylized rose and patterned squares motif has been widely adapted, and can be duplicated for a variety of interior decorating uses. Here, the theme has been executed in stained glass for a charming accent window.*

BELOW: *The stained glass wall and skylights in the living room of the Meyer May House, designed by Frank Lloyd Wright, travel the full length of the space. The windows take as their theme geometric plant forms, and throw intricate shadows across the carpet according to the season.*

with painted fairylike creatures; these windows tell marvelous stories. Charles Lamb Studios in New York City rivaled the stained glass of Tiffany, and Elbert Hubbard sent the versatile Roycroft artisan Dard Hunter to study there. Upon his return to East Aurora, Hunter designed charming windows and lanterns in stained and leaded glass for various Roycroft buildings.

Frank Lloyd Wright did not physically make the fabulous windows he designed. However, these windows and the few desk and table lamps that he had made to his specifications have brought some of the highest recorded prices. Wright drew upon geometric forms and stylized renderings of Native American designs for his art glass. These themes blended well with his Prairie-style homes, which owed their horizontal forms to the spreading flatlands of the Midwest.

The architects Greene and Greene also had their stained glass windows made by artisans in accordance to their designs. Their motifs are typically more flowing than Wright's, and their colors more subtle and elegant. The doors of the Gamble House comprise a masterwork, and surely are among the most photographed stained glass pieces in the world.

Collecting art pottery, tile, and glass is a rewarding hobby, and can add to the look of your Arts and Crafts home. Remember that unique, original pieces should be used alone to highlight the decorating scheme. You can also create pleasing vignettes with several pieces—keep in mind that an odd number of objects is more pleasing to the eye, particularly when an assortment of heights and shapes is grouped together. Don't forget to anchor fragile objects in order to protect them. Products such as Quake Hold (the brand name for a claylike substance that anchors objects but never hardens) make pottery a safe investment, even in earthquake country. It is also prudent to use a product such as Quake Hold if you have children or pets. Cracked or broken pottery and tile can sometimes be repaired so the damaged area is nearly invisible, but art glass is impossible to mend.

The fragile nature of art pottery, tile, and glass should not keep you from incorporating them into your Arts and Crafts home. These accessories are the jewels that make an Arts and Crafts interior glow with refinement.

ABOVE: *Stained glass Arts and Crafts lanterns like this lovely Japanese-influenced design are reproduced by several companies today. Glass in muted colors and with themes drawn from nature are the most appropriate choices for an Arts and Crafts decor.*

CHAPTER

9

ARTWORK
AND
ACCESSORIES

PRECEDING PAGES: *Embroidery and appliqué work are two of the decorative embellishments appropriate to the Arts and Crafts style. While excessive ornament was frowned upon, needleworked items using the favorite motifs of the movement added beauty and comfort to the home. Stylized tulips, daisies, pine cones and needles, gingko leaves, roses, and grapes are but a few of the popular patterns that grace textiles of the era.*

Artwork and accessories may seem like small items relative to the home's overall size, yet many serious collectors put more money into these objects than they do into the house or its furnishings. Pottery, artwork, metalware, and books are often a collector's primary focus, while the house to be decorated may be modest and not even of the Arts and Crafts style.

When it comes to decorating with artwork and accessories, there are several things you need to remember. Harmony and the relationship among objects in a room, along with effective use of color and lighting, are particularly important aspects of Arts and Crafts interior decorating.

Without the appropriate colors and spacious room arrangement, the Arts and Crafts style can seem oppressive and dark. Simplifying a room by removing clutter is an Arts and Crafts rule to live by. This is not to suggest that each surface must feature only one object, despite the fact that the style is often photographed and presented in this manner. A mantel, side table, or even a windowseat might hold a collection of art pottery, glass, or metalware. Groupings of compatible prints are often more pleasing to the eye than are individual pieces, although fine paintings usually deserve single billing in important locations.

Today's lifestyle produces a lot of "stuff." Your first step in creating a true Arts and Crafts look is to clean out the unattractive and the useless. Follow the advice of William Morris: "Have nothing in your home that is not functional or that you do not believe to be beautiful."

Naturally, the weeding out process can be problematic, and sometimes even frightening. What to do with useless and ugly mementos? The porcelain bird your mother-in-law gave you, the children's artwork (if it's good, frame it properly and display it proudly!), or the menu from that restaurant in Georgetown? Create a study collection, museum style, in a back hall, mudroom, or laundry room. You will visit them often. A shelf around the top of that room, with items arranged neatly, can make any trinket look sharp.

OPPOSITE: *A blend of American and British furniture and accessories, including pre-Raphaelite artwork, helps to create a comfortable yet elegant country feel. The mirror frame of polished copper with inset tile is from Liberty of London. This handsome room, more elaborately decorated than its American counterparts, is eclectic Arts and Crafts.*
LEFT: *The quintessential Craftsman interior, Gustav Stickley's own home at Craftsman Farms, is filled with furniture and accessories from his workshops. This pared down setting looks comfortable without being cluttered; the graceful lines of well-designed furniture and one appliquéd pillow are the only ornament necessary in this serene space.*

ARTWORK

RTWORK FROM THE Arts and Crafts era or reproductions of period artwork is essential to the decor if your desire is to achieve a cohesive scheme. While contemporary artwork can be harmonious, it is the paintings, prints, photographs, and posters of the era that convey the true character of the Arts and Crafts Movement.

Plein air paintings—landscapes done out of doors—are the perfect complement for an Arts and Crafts interior because they use nature and regionalism as their focus, two important themes of the Arts and Crafts philosophy. Today, artists like Tom Bojanowski and Brian Stewart once again paint local landscapes out of doors, in the manner of period painters Maurice Braun of the Point Loma community in San Diego, California, and Alex Fournier of Roycroft in East Aurora, New York. Plein air paintings captured nature at varying times of the day—dawn, midday, sunset, on moonglow—and in different seasons throughout the year. These landscape paintings brought nature into the home and put both the artist and the viewer in touch with the outdoors. In keeping with the Arts and Crafts ideal of the artist being involved with his work all the way through the process, the framing of these pieces were historically (and are today) done by the artist himself or by a local artisan colleague.

BELOW: *William Keith's oil on canvas murals depict the early California scenery. Landscape paintings are the perfect complement to log cabins and other rustic Arts and Crafts architectural styles, bringing indoors the natural beauty that both the building and the artwork celebrate.*

The Arts and Crafts societies of the day exhibited the work of painters, print-makers, photographers, and craftspeople together, emphasizing their connectedness not only with each other but also with their buyers. The integrity of the artisan—the love, warmth, and joy every good artist works into a piece—is passed on to the consumer and becomes an heirloom of the next generation.

Museum houses in England, such as Wightwick Manor, Craigside, and Standen, are full of authentic paintings by pre-Raphaelite artists depicting scenes from ancient mythology, the Bible, and the Arthurian legends. While original works by well-known painters such as Dante Gabriel Rosetti or Edward Burne-Jones are rare and expensive, quality prints are available at the Victoria and Albert Museum in London and the Delaware Art Museum in the United States. Properly framed, these prints can bring an elegant Morris-inspired bedroom to life.

The English graphic artist Aubrey Beardsley and the well-known Viennese artist Gustav Klimt are not thought of as being part of the Arts and Crafts genre, but in fact they epitomize the philosophy of the movement. Their cutting-edge designs and subjects flew in the face of the established traditions and styles. Klimt's kaleidoscopic compositions mixed modern and traditional styles, and almost always featured seductive and beautiful women as a central theme. During the Arts and Crafts era, Vienna was in the throes of a final creative salute, a cultural flowering that married illusion with reality.

Like Klimt, Beardsley was devoted to the erotic portrayal of the femme fatale. Indeed, Sigmund Freud, with his unabashed approach to sexuality, set the stage for

A B O V E : *Landscape paintings were common in bungalows and other Arts and Crafts houses, and were often given pride of place above the mantel. This mural is set off by a fine array of art pottery; the Roseville Mostique pottery on the left dates from 1914 and is highly prized by collectors.*

RIGHT: *A repoussé polished copper frame sets off the medieval-themed painting and is the perfect accessory for a mantel of similar design. In the tradition of William Morris, this vignette captures the simple elegance that is the epitome of the Arts and Crafts ideal.*

this revolution. The new science of psychoanalysis asserted sexuality as normal and natural, and these artists' portrayals followed suit.

Posters and other graphics are also collectible and are striking if properly placed. Kitchens, family rooms, and sun porches are perfect settings for stylized, colorful poster prints. Recent Arts and Crafts exhibitions have yielded marvelous promotion posters, just as their early cousins once did. Inexpensively framed, they create a worthy collection on their own.

Vintage calendar prints of turn-of-the-century Arts and Crafts artists are worth acquiring, and new prints are available. Other types of prints, including wood or linoleum block prints and silk-screen images, are also beautiful additions to the Arts and Crafts home. The works of Arthur Wesley Dow and Yoshida Hiroshi are gorgeous and still somewhat affordable. Currently, Roycroft Renaissance artists Kathy West (block prints) and Dorothy Markert (silk screen) are producing collectible, charming, and reasonably priced pieces.

PHOTOGRAPHY

PHOTOGRAPHY WAS A NEW ART form during the Arts and Crafts era, and a soft and romantic photographic style of the period known as "pictorialist" or "tonalist" continues to be very appealing to collectors. While prices for original pictorialist photos are escalating as appreciation for them grows, they are still available.

Another growing segment of the collectible photography market is antique photos of Native Americans, a popular and romantic subject in the latter half of the nineteenth century. The photographic portraits of many indigenous peoples taken by Edward Curtis are handsome additions to offices and dens but may prove overpowering in other areas of the house. Generally, several editions of such prints were made, and it pays, as it does with all artwork and antiques, to go to a reputable dealer. The "jumble" or "white elephant" sale still offers the best bargains if you are truly knowledgeable and have a good eye.

SCULPTURE

BRONZES AND METAL COMPOSITION editions of caryatids, griffins, gargoyles, and other gothic creatures find appropriately majestic, yet comfortable, homes in bookcases and on small occasional tables. Frank Lloyd Wright often punctuated his decor with reproductions of ancient sculptures, the *Winged Victory of Samothrace* being his favorite. Reproductions of ancient or medieval pieces are often available at reasonable costs, and can link your Arts and Crafts home to the original philosophies and style of the movement.

Frederick Remington's well-known sculptures of cowboys and Native Americans can be stunning if one practices restraint. Use this theme sparingly, and only in a room with simple Mission or rustic furniture.

BOOKS

BOOKS CAN BE ACQUIRED at two levels. First is the growing library of books available about the Arts and Crafts period—a handsome coffee-table book can in itself be a work of art. The information these books provide is invaluable; and they add to the enjoyment of your home, which should be a place of exceptional comfort and pleasure. Private press books and magazines from the period, such as those printed at Roycroft or Kelmscott, are valuable both

A B O V E : *Beautifully bound books were a point of pride in the Arts and Crafts home. Original Arts and Crafts volumes as well as books about the period make fine collections for the enthusiast.*

for their content and as a good investment in your art collection. They are still affordable and are often a handsome way to decorate the living room or library. Antique and reproduction Roycroft mottoes are framable in new or old Roycroft frames. The originals once hung in households and offices around the world.

LINENS

ARTS AND CRAFTS-ERA LINENS are highly decorative and are easy to use as dresser scarves, as doilies on side tables, under lamps, and as table runners. Embroidery and appliqué in soft colors such as lilac, pink, and pale gray were chiefly worked on plain fabrics such as unbleached muslin or linen. As in other crafts of the era, typical designs included natural forms such as flowers and leaves, and the Glasgow rose was counted a particular favorite. These designs transformed textiles from pillows and tablecloths to portieres and bed hangings. Superb examples of antique textiles are delicate and best displayed as framed artwork.

ABOVE: *Crewelwork was a favorite adornment for Arts and Crafts bed linens. The designs were available in kits and they would also have been published in women's magazines of the day. Today, both finished pieces and kits are available.*

RIGHT: *A properly laid table included appliquéd or embroidered table runners, napkins, and tall candlesticks. Plant motifs were popular, and graced table linens, bed coverings, and throw pillows. The gingko leaf design on this table runner was originally published in* The Craftsman *in about 1910 and is still being produced today.*
OPPOSITE: *Pillows of embroidered linen mixed with nature-themed prints form a cozy collection on the settee. Fine rugs, like this colorful example, are best hung on the wall, a treatment that recalls the tapestries of medieval times. An assortment of patterns can work together if similar colors are mixed and the rules of scale are observed.*

Wonderful reproductions of Arts and Crafts designs have been created by Dianne Ayres, Arts and Crafts Textiles, and others, so linens and pillows are easy to incorporate into your home. The designs are available in kit form, enabling you to participate—in true Arts and Crafts fashion—in making your own accessories. Remember that textile pieces help to give the color punctuation and balance that is so essential to the creation of an Arts and Crafts interior.

METALWARE

PERHAPS THE FAIREST AND FINEST of all Arts and Crafts accessories is the metalware. Whether bronze, silver, brass, or copper, metal's rich patina or polished glory adds a glint of hard surface to an interior like seed pearls on a wedding gown.

No other craft produced by the Roycrofters is as prized as their copper work. All of their metal pieces use copper as a base, though it may be plated with silver or brass. Because bookmaking was the primary craft at Roycroft, all sorts of desk and library accoutrements were produced, along with vases, candlesticks, fruit bowls, and trays. Viennese-style pieces with silver accents or cutouts were made for only a few years, and are the most beautiful and rare of all. Roycroft hardware, such as hinges and drawer and cabinet pulls, was produced in the attractive medieval style.

Robert Jarvie, Dirk Van Erp, and the artisans of Gustav Stickley's shops were superb metalworkers, and their designs are those most often reproduced today. Their vases, lamp bases, lanterns, and candlesticks are of excellent design and workmanship. Cutouts, such as hearts, are a popular feature in Stickley's designs.

ABOVE: *A fine collection of copper chargers by both English and European craftsmen and -women grace this hanging oak plate rack. The scene is softly lit by a pair of Charles Rohlfs candlesticks wrought of copper and wood.*
RIGHT: *This Liberty of London sideboard is home to a collection of English and European pewter, with makers that include Kayserin, Liberty, and W.M.F.*

English copper was, and is still, always polished, unlike the American work, which was allowed to acquire a patina over time. The British are only now beginning to polish the pewter work of Archibald Knox, Christopher Dresser, and C.R. Ashbee, which had long been left in its darkened state.

Silver pieces, were part of the Arts and Crafts array of metalware. In the United States the Gorham Company and Louis Comfort Tiffany made excellent pieces; Liberty of London and Bing's La Maison de l'Art Nouveau in Paris also carried fine Arts and Crafts silverware. Like copper and other metals, silverware was usually hammered, to avoid the too-perfect finish that Arts and Crafts designers deplored. Art silver is always polished.

The Wiener Werkstätte was known for the excellent quality of its metal art. Koloman Moser and Josef Hoffmann both made memorable pieces, many of which demonstrated their affinity with the work of C.R. Mackintosh, particularly in the use of pierced squares.

Accessories are the finishing touches that make a house a home, so include the decorative flourishes that make your interior sparkle with personality and charm. Embroidered linens and pillows, finely wrought copper candlesticks, vintage photography, or a collection of Arts and Crafts books—no matter what you choose to collect and display, these objects of beauty and functionality are sure to enhance your home.

CHRONOLOGY OF THE ARTS AND CRAFTS MOVEMENT

IT TOOK TWENTY YEARS for the Arts and Crafts Movement to develop in England, and it took twenty years at the end of the movement to fade away in the United States between the World Wars. The time of most intense creativity was the dozen years on either side of the turn of the century. As with all creative movements, the highest productivity followed the innovative years. During this time of commercial prosperity, the key players departed due either to bankruptcy, death, or despair, while imitators of lesser quality often followed and flourished.

1834   Birth of William Morris.

1841   *The True Principles of Pointed or Christian Architecture* published by A.W.N. Pugin.

1848   Pre-Raphaelite Brotherhood formed and first Pre-Raphaelite works exhibited.

1849   John Ruskin publishes *Seven Lamps of Architecture.*

1851   London: The "Great Exhibition" (the Great Exhibition of the Works of Industry of All Nations), held under the direction of the Prince Consort and Sir Henry Cole. Allegedly visited by Morris, then aged seventeen, who was nauseated by the tasteless and materialistic display.

Stones of Venice published by Ruskin.

1856   Owen Jones's *The Grammar of Ornament* published, the first book to have full-color plates printed by chromolithography.

1859   Planning and building of William and Jane Morris's Red House by Philip Webb at Upton in Kent (decorated by Webb, Burne-Jones, and Rossetti).

1861   Morris, Marshall, Faulkner & Co. founded to provide the type of furniture so conspicuously lacking in the mid–nineteenth century—solidly constructed and without superfluous ornament.

1866   Morris & Co. undertakes two important commissions: the decoration of the Green Dining Room at the South Kensington Museum and the Armoury and Tapestry at St. James' Palace.

1874   Morris begins his experiments with fabric design.

1875   Formation of Liberty & Co.

1876   Philadephia: Centennial Exposition.

1879   L.C. Tiffany & Co., Associated Artists founded in New York with the cooperation of Candace Wheeler and the Society of Decorative Art.

1880   Rookwood Pottery founded by Mary Louise McLaughlin in Cincinnati, Ohio.

First practical electric lights are developed and the streets of New York are lit by them.

1882–3 L.C. Tiffany & Co., Associated Artists decorates the White House.

1888   Arts and Crafts Exposition Society is organized in London.

The Guild of Handicraft is founded in London by Charles Ashbee.

1889   Hull House is founded by Jane Addams and Ellen Gates Starr in Chicago.

Frank Lloyd Wright builds his home in Oak Park, Illinois.

1890   Establishment of William Morris's Kelmscott Press.

1893   Chicago: World's Columbian Exposition.

The Studio begins publication in England.

Charles and Henry Greene begin their architectural practice in Pasadena, California.

1894   Elbert Hubbard visits the Kelmscott Press in England, possibly meeting William Morris.

1895   Elbert Hubbard establishes Roycroft Press and begins publication of *The Philistine,* which is published until his death in 1915.

Samuel Bing publishes his *La Culture Artistique en Amerique,* the result of his observations made during a trip to the United States in 1893 to visit the Chicago World's Fair. At the end of the same year, he alters his shop, which had previously concentrated on the sale of objects imported from the Far East, to make it a showcase for modern designers and craftspeople. It is now known as La Maison de l'Art Nouveau.

Newcomb College Pottery is established in New Orleans.

Chalk and Chisel Club, the first Arts and Crafts society in the United States, is organized in Minneapolis.

1896   Death of William Morris.

First issue of *House Beautiful* is published in Chicago.

The Guild of Arts & Crafts is formed in San Francisco.

1897   Roycroft Print Shop under construction.

Boston Society of Arts & Crafts and Chicago Arts & Crafts Society are established.

C.R. Mackintosh first undertakes the designing, decorating, and furnishing of a number of tearooms in Glasgow for the Misses Cranston.

1898 The artists' colony at Darmstadt is set up by the Grand Duke of Hesse.

Furniture designs commissioned by M. H. Baillie Scott and C.R. Ashbee and made by the Guild of Handicraft.

Roycroft begins to make furniture for its shop.

Gustav Stickley travels to Europe and upon his return begins Gustav Stickley and Co. in Syracuse, New York.

1898–9 Liberty's Cymric silver range established. The most prolific and consistently used designer was the Manxman Archibald Knox.

Adelaide Alsop Robineau begins publication of *Keramic Studio* in Syracuse, New York.

The Roycroft Chapel is built.

The Boston Society of Arts & Crafts holds its second exhibition.

1901 Buffalo: Pan-American Exposition; Stickley and McHugh introduce their line of furniture to the public. Also exhibiting are Charles Rohlfs, L.C. Tiffany, Gorham, Grueby, Newcomb Pottery, Volkmar, and Adelaide Robineau. Gold medals go to Grueby, Rookwood, and Tiffany; silver to Tiffany and Newcomb; bronze to Volkmar.

The Craftsman first published by Gustav Stickley in Syracuse, New York.

The Arden Community is founded by William Price and others in Arden, Delaware; it lasts only one year.

House & Garden begins publication in Philadelphia.

Roycroft begins production of furniture.

Frank Lloyd Wright delivers his lecture "The Art and Craft of the Machine" at Hull House in Chicago.

1901–02 Roycroft Print Shop constructed.

1902 The Morris Society begins in Chicago.

A major exhibition of Arts and Crafts is held at the Craftsman Building in Syracuse, New York.

The Roycroft Copper Shop opens.

The Craftsman Home Builders Club is formed.

1903 Roycroft Inn opens.

1904 Louisiana Purchase International Exposition takes place in St. Louis, exhibiting much of the Arts and Crafts work produced in America.

1905 Ernest Batchelder visits Ashbee's Guild at Chipping Camden, England, and works in the shops there.

1907 The National League of Handicrafts, Boston, is formed.

1908 The Gamble House, designed by Greene & Greene, is built in Pasadena, California.

Dirk van Erp opens his copper shop in San Francisco.

1909 Guild of Handicraft is disbanded.

Rose Valley Community goes bankrupt.

Craftsman Homes is first published by Stickley.

Frank Lloyd Wright undertakes his first West Coast commission.

Frank Lloyd Wright leaves for Europe.

C.R. Ashbee visits California and meets the Greenes, comparing their adaptation of Japanese architectural features favorably with the work of Frank Lloyd Wright.

The Bungalow magazine is first published by Henry Wilson in Los Angeles.

1910 Frank Lloyd Wright's Ausgefuehrte Bauten und Entwerfe published in Berlin with a foreword by Ashbee. That year, he stays with Ashbee in Chipping Camden.

Gustav Stickley, editor of *The Craftsman*, admits that he has never built the Craftsman houses, which he designed and published, and that he knew that their cost would be much greater than his estimates. Circulation of *The Craftsman* begins to drop.

1912 Archibald Knox visits Philadelphia and New York.

More Craftsman Homes is published by Stickley.

Construction of the Roycroft Powerhouse.

1913 The Grove Park Inn is built in Asheville, North Carolina, furnished by Roycroft (the largest commission they ever had).

1915 Elbert and Alice Hubbard perish on the *Lusitania*, May 7.

Gustav Stickley declares bankruptcy.

San Francisco: Panama-Pacific International Exposition.

San Diego: Panama-Californian Exposition.

1916 Last issue of *The Craftsman*, October.

1917 L.C. Tiffany goes bankrupt.

1919 The Bauhaus founded in April in Weimar by Walter Gropius, who had studied architecture under Peter Behrens.

1920s Heyday of Roycroft under Elbert Hubbard II. Roycroft Copper Shop at peak production.

1926 Cranbrook Institute designed by Eric and Elliel Saranen; opens in Ann Arbor, Michigan.

1930s The Great Depression precipitates a winding down of the still-producing Arts and Crafts studios, shops, and enterprises. The few houses still being built in the United States until World War II are often bungalow designs.

1933 Arthurdale, a Works Projects Administration craft community in West Virginia, is planned as a result of the National Industrial Recovery Act of 1933. It is presided over by Eleanor Roosevelt and aided by Louis Howe, FDR's right-hand man.

GLOSSARY

arched apron The curved bottom of a bookcase, china cabinet, or the like, often used to soften a rectilinear design.

Art Nouveau A design style of flowing curvilinear lines inspired by vines, flowers, and other natural elements and employed within the Arts and Crafts Movement in Spain, France, Belgium, and Eastern Europe.

attenuated Overlengthened, like the tall backs of chairs by Charles Rennie Mackintosh and Frank Lloyd Wright.

clinker brick A brick that has been purposely burned too much in the kiln, causing a slag effect. Used in West Coast American Arts and Crafts architecture.

even arm settle A wood frame couch, usually of oak, with a back support that joins the arms in an unbroken line; also called a crib settle.

German silver Nickel (not silver at all!) used during the Arts and Crafts period as an accent on copper and other metals, especially for vases, candlesticks, and lanterns.

hand-hammered/spun A method of manufacture, especially of copper, during the Arts and Crafts period. A piece of copper was hammered, entirely by hand, over a wooden form or, with wood, the piece would be spun on a lathe.

hoosier A work station cabinet for the new 1900s Arts and Crafts kitchen. It held a flour sifter and baking supplies and had a pull-out enameled counter work space.

inglenook A room within a room around a fireplace, usually created by two benches facing each other at right angles to the hearth.

Jungenstil The German name for Art Nouveau, literally translated as "young" or "new" style.

lantern Antiquated name, revived by Arts and Crafts artisans, for a hanging light fixture. Arts and Crafts lanterns were made of copper and mica, or of brass or wood with stained-glass inserts.

mica A naturally occurring mineral often used as a lampshade material. Laid in very thin sheets, it is usually covered with orange shellac.

Morris chair A type of adjustable reclining armchair first designed by Philip Webb of Morris & Co. in the United Kingdom in the 1870s and adapted by most American Arts and Crafts furniture artisans.

mortise and tenon joint The coming together of a projecting piece of wood, called a tenon, and an opening, usually a rectangle cut into a piece of wood. The tenon can be exposed and "keyed" with a third piece of wood to secure the two pieces without nails or glue.

patina A film, usually greenish, that develops over time on copper or bronze. It can also be created artificially by adding chemicals to copper, brass, or bronze.

pergola An exterior structure consisting of parallel colonnades supporting an open roof of cross rafters or vines.

peristyle A long, open, columned, covered walkway; in the tradition of ancient Greece a peristyle was where philosophers would meet. The most famous peristyle in the United States is at the Roycroft Inn.

pilaster A portion of a rectangular column attached to a wall; in Arts and Crafts houses these were often used in interiors as visual dividers.

plein air A landscape painting done out of doors; literally translated as "plain air," this was the prevalent landscape style of the early twentieth century Arts and Crafts artists.

quartersawn A method of cutting wood wherein the cut is parallel to the medullary rays, not across them. This produces a "ray flake" that creates a striping effect in lumber, especially oak.

shed dormer A dormer with a roof that slopes in the same direction as the roof, very common in bungalows.

slag glass Opaque glass, usually of several colors blended; used as a shade material in lighting fixtures.

tabouret A small table or stool; also spelled tabourette.

Major Arts & Crafts Antique Shops and Galleries

Accardi & Bennett
145 Chambers St.
New York, NY 10007
(212) 962-3311

Acorn Antiques
Craftsman Gallery
48 Route 214
Phoenicia, NY 12464
(914) 688-2100

American Art Pottery
Jay Dubiel
P.O. Box 926
Halifax, VA 24558
(804) 575-5781

American Arts & Crafts Gallery
Bob Berman
4456 Main Street
Olde Manayunk, PA 19027
(215) 482-8667
(610) 566-1516

American Decorative Arts
Chris Kennedy
3 Olive St.
Northhampton, MA 01060
(413) 584-6804
1 (800) 366-3376

American Furnishings
1423A Grandview
Columbus, OH 43212
(614) 488-7263

Antique Articles
Sandie Fowler,
Wendy Harvey
1 Hilltop Rd.
Billerica, MA 01820-2307
(508) 663-8083 Ph/Fax

Antique Underground
247 W. Fayette St.
Syracuse, NY
(315) 472-5510

Art Moderne Antiques
John Hermann,
John Jung
P.O. Box 72
San Antonio, FL 33576
(904) 588-3437

Arts and Crafts Gallery
811 Royal St.
New Orleans, LA 70116
(504) 524-6918

ASG Antiques
George and Karin Look
Rt. 2, Box 66
Berkeley, WV 25411
(304) 258-4037
(703) 683-3871

Joshua Baer & Co.
Classic American Indian Art
116½ E. Palace Ave.
Santa Fe, NM 87501
(505) 988-8944

Big Two-Hearted
Ned Duke, Greg Klinger
604 Bridge St.
Charlevoix, MI 49720
(616) 547-3474
313) 485-2444

Blue Moon Antiques
Mark Millard
1129 Lawndale Drive
Menasha, WI 54952
(414) 729-9368

Jean Bragg Antiques
3901 Magazine St.
New Orleans, LA 70115
(504) 895-7375

Merrilee Brown Antiques
32 Lawrence Rd.
Hyde Park, NY 12538-2427
(914) 229-7322

Richard Caggiano Antiques
114 Partition St.
Saugerties, NY 12477
(914) 679-7561

Cathers and Dembrosky
43 East Tenth St.
New York, NY 10003
(201) 894-8140

Cavanaugh Antiques
271 S. Ardenwood Dr.
Baton Rouge, LA 70806
(504) 924-4441

Chenonceau Antiques
Andrea Schneider
2314 18th St., NW
Washington, DC 20009
(202) 667-1651

Cherry Tree Antiques
1045 Park Ridge Road
Hillsboro, MO 63050
(314) 968-0708

Circa 1910 Antiques
Jim & Jill West
7206 Melrose Avenue
Los Angeles, CA 90046
(213) 965-1910

Circa 87
The Antique & Artisan Centre
69 Jefferson St.
Stamford, CT
(203) 968-6485

Classic Interiors and Antiques
Doug and Paula White
2042 N. Rio Grande Avenue
Orlando, FL 32804
(407) 839-0004

Cooper House Antiques
P.O. Box 586
Woodstock, NY 12498
(914) 679-7561

Craftsman Style
1453 Fourth St.
Santa Monica, CA 90401
(310) 393-1468

Dalton's
Debbie Goldwein Rudd &
David Rudd
1931 James St.
Syracuse, NY 13206
(315) 463-1568

Geoffrey Diner
1730 21st St.
Washington, DC 20009
(202) 483-5005

William Doyle Galleries
175 E. 87th St.
New York, NY 10128
(212) 427-2730
Fax: (212) 369-0892

Edwards Antiques
Tom and Cindy Edwards
89 Hillsboro St.
Pittsboro, NC 27312
(919) 542-5649

Michael Fitzsimmons
Decorative Arts
311 W. Superior St.
Chicago, IL 60610
(312) 787-0496

Flury & Company
Photography Gallery
322 First Ave. S.
Seattle, WA 98104
(206) 587-0260

Fordham & Nelson
3267 Bee Caves Rd.
Suite 107-244
Austin, TX 78746
(512) 930-0124

Pearce R. Fox
St. Davids, PA
(610) 688-3678

Ann and Leo Gallarano
Rt. 2 Box 66
Berkeley Springs, WV 25411
(304) 258-4037

Gallery 532 Soho
Karen Wellikoff
117 Wooster Street
New York, NY 10012
(212) 219-1327
Fax: (212) 219-1810

Tim Gleason Gallery
77 Sullivan St.
New York, NY 10012
(212) 966-5777

Heartwood
Don Marek
956 Cherry Street
Grand Rapids, MI 49506
(616) 454-1478

The Heintz Art Metal Shop
David H. Surgan
328 Flatbush Ave. #123
Brooklyn, NY 11238
(718) 638-3768

Hilding & Larson Emporium
Vivian A. Highberg
1741 Partridge Run Road
Pittsburgh, PA 15241
(412) 854-1421

House of Hubbard
Linda Hubbard Brady
541 Fillmore Avenue
East Aurora, NY 14052
(716) 652-0213

House of Orange
Arthur van der Beek
& John Zanakis
Alameda, CA 94501
(510) 523-3378

Jandon Antiques
108 North Rd.
Chelmsford, MA 01824

JMW Co.
Jim Messineo
144 Lincoln Street
Boston, MA 02111
(617) 338-9097

Preston Jordan
P.O. Box 55
Madison, NJ 07940
(201) 593-4866

Kylloe Antiques
Ralph Kylloe
P.O. Box 669
Lake George, NY 12845-0669

LePoulaille
Bob Berman
441 S. Jackson St.
Media, PA 19063
(610) 566-1516

Lifetime Arts and Crafts
Gallery
7115 Melrose Ave.
Los Angeles, CA 90046
(213) 939-7441

Isak Lindenauer Antiques
4143 19th Street
San Francisco, CA 94114
(415) 552-6436

George & Karin Look
608 Johnston Pl.
Alexandria, VA 22301
(703) 683-3871

Lower's Furniture &
Cabinetry
Bill & Chris Lower
425 Floral Ave.
Ithaca, NY 14840
(607) 277-4769

Jim Mall
907 W. Ainslie St.
Chicago, IL 60640
(312) 561-9732

Mayfield Antiques of
Grand Rapids
445 Bridge St.
Grand Rapids, MI 49504
(616) 451-3430
Fax: (616) 235-3113

McCormack & Co.
Tony McCormack
245 Bird Key Dr.
Sarasota, FL 34236
(941) 952-1244

The Metal Man
Raymond Groll
Box 421 Station A
Flushing, NY 11358
(718) 463-0059

Mission Era Ltd.
106 Orchard St.
Belmont, MA 02178
(617) 484-4800
Fax: (617) 864-3862

Mission Oak Antiques
378 Meigs St.
Rochester, NY 14607
(716) 442-2480

Mission Oak Shop
Jerry Cohen
123 Main Street
Putnam, CT 06260
(203) 928-6662

Mission Position
1122 Washington
Hoboken, NJ 07030
(201) 656-3398

Mission Possible
Affordable Arts & Crafts
5516 Connecticut Ave. N.W.
Washington, DC 20015
(202) 363-6897
Fax (202) 363-7388

The Mission Shop
Gary Reynolds
220 Beach Drive NE
St. Petersburg, FL 33701
(813) 896-6713

Modern Design
5309 Jackson St.
Omaha, NE 68106
(402) 551-5018

Jack Moore
59 E. Colorado Blvd.
Pasadena, CA 91105
(818) 577-7746

Morseberg Galleries
Plein-Air Paintings
9089 Santa Monica Blvd.
Los Angeles, CA 90069
(310) 273-5207
(800) 707-4278

1904 Antiques and Design
Craig Litherland
1226 SE Lexington
Portland, OR 97202

Old City Mission
162 North 3rd St.
Philadelphia, PA 19106
(215) 413-3040

Our Mission Antiques
Leslie and Sydelle Sher
525 Hidden Pines Tr.
Holly, MI 48442
(810) 634-7612

Ouroboros Art Pottery
Art Antique Village
10203 Chamberlayne Rd.
Mechanicsville, VA 23111
mailing address:
1402 Confederate Ave.
Richmond, VA 23227
(804) 730-8004

Bob Palko
Weller Pottery
502 Mapleway
Houston, TX 77015
(713) 453-3273

Pasternak's Emporium
Cary Pasternak
2515 Morse St.
Houston, TX 77019
(713) 528-3808

Pastime Furniture
Laurence R. Green
609 Colorade Ave.
Stuart, FL 34994
(561) 287-6230

Peter-Roberts Antiques
Robert Melita, Peter Smorto
134 Spring St.
New York, NY 10012
(212) 226-4777

Pete's Pots
Pete Maloney
5028 Rockborough Tr.
Norcross, GA 30071
(770) 446-1419

The Plastic Arts
Andrew T. Lopez
P.O. Box 1294
Jackson, MI 49204
(517) 782-9910

The Pottery Place
Betty Powell
P.O. Box 571
Worthington, OH 43085
(614) 885-1962 Phone/Fax

David Rago Arts & Crafts
Gallery
17 S. Main St.
Lambertville, NJ 08530
(609) 397-9374

Red Accordian 20th Century
Design
3421 Grand Avenue
Oakland, CA 94610
(510) 834-1661

Thomas Reynolds Gallery
(415) 441-4093

Larry and Roslyn Rose
Rookwood Dealers
P.O. Box 9215
Bartonia, NY 10954
(914) 634-7801

Roycroft Shops
Robert Rust & Kitty Turgeon
31 S. Grove St.
East Aurora, N.Y. 14052
(716) 652-3333

Terry Seger
Stickley Brothers Copper
880 Foxcreek Lane
Cincinatti, OH 45233
(513) 941-8689

Silverman's Selected Antiques
10924 Cinderella
Dallas, TX 75229
(214) 351-4851

Barbara M. Smith
P.O. Box 94
Canaan, NH 03741
(603) 523-9114

Colin C. Smith
5309 Jackson St.
Omaha, NE 68106-5018
(402) 551-5018

So Rare Galleries
Edith Crawford
701 Smithfield
Pittsburgh, PA 15290
(412) 281-5150

South Street Antiques
Roulhac B. Toledano
Charlottesville, VA 22902
(804) 295-2449

Split Personality - Leah Roland
P.O. Box 419,
Leonia, NJ 07605
(201) 947-1535

Steptoe & Wife Antiques Ltd.
322 Geary Avenue
Toronto, Ontario,
Canada M6H2C7
(416) 530-4200
Fax (416) 530-4666
(800) 461-0060
steptoe@terraport.net;
www.terraport.net/steptoe

Gary Stuncius
P.O. Box 1374
Lakewood, NJ 08701
(800) 272-2529

Bruce Szopo
3860 Ellamae
Oakland, MI 48363
(313) 652-7652

Phil Taylor Antiques
224 Fox-Sauk Road
Ottumwa, IA 52501
(515) 682-7492 (shop)
(515) 682-3318

Steven Thomas, Inc.
Box 41
Woodstock, VT 05091
(802) 457-1764 Phone/Fax
(800) 781-8028

Threshold Antiques at
Massachusetts Antiques
Co-op
100 Fetton St.
Waltham, MA
(617) 893-8893

John Toomey
818 North Boulevard
Oak Park, IL 60302
(312) 383-5234

Towpath Antiques
Ron and Judy Truex
512 West Valley View Avenue
Hackettstown, NJ 07840
(908) 852-7689

Treadway Gallery, Inc.
Fine Arts, Antiques
2029 Madison Road
Cincinnati, OH 45208
(513) 321-64742
Fax (513) 871-7722

20th Century Art and Design
Steve Schonek
P.O. Box 56
Newport, MN 55055
(612) 459-2980

20th Century Consortium
1004 Westport Rd.
Kansas City, MO 64111
(816) 931-0986

20th Century Unlimited
Philip Gabe and Patricia
Edwards
3320 Troup Hwy. #285
Tyler, TX 75713

The Verlangieri Gallery
American Arts & Crafts
P.O. Box 844
Cambria, CA 93428
(805) 927-4428

Voorhees Craftsman
Santa Monica Antiques Market
1607 Lincoln Blvd.
Santa Monica, CA 90404

Berkeley Antiques
1370 10th Street
Berkeley, CA 94710

Woodsbridge Antiques
Norman & Debby Weinstein
P.O. Box #239
Yonkers, NY 10705
(914) 963-7671

Lamps and Lighting Fixtures

Antiques Interiors West, Inc.
212 Homer St.
Palo Alto, CA 94301
(415) 324-1339

Arroyo Craftsmen
4509 Little John St.
Baldwin Park, CA 91706
(818) 960-9411

Aurora Studios
Michael Adams
109 Main St.
Putnam, CT 06260
(860) 928-6662
Specializes in Gustav Stickley
and Van Erp reproductions

Karl Berry Studio
263-267 Douglass St.
Brooklyn, NY 11217
(718) 596-1419

Brass Light Gallery
131 S. 1st St.
Milwaukee, WI 53204
(414) 271-8300
Fax: (414) 271-7755
(800) 243-9595

Classic Tiffany
3628 Pennsylvania Avenue S.
Minneapolis, MN 55426
(612) 930-9210
Fax: (612) 935-4761

Collier Lighting
3100 Kerner Blvd.
San Rafael, CA 94901-5440
(415) 454-6672

Conant Custom Brass
Norris A. Trombly
266-270 Pine Street
Burlington, VT 05401
(802) 658-4482
Fax (802) 864-5914
(800) 832-4482
Purveyors of fine lighting
and decorative metalwork

Christian Fields
P.O. Box 87
Frankfort, MI 49635
(616) 352-6106

FMG Design
Frank Glapa
2601 West Farwell
Chicago, IL 60645
(773) 761-2957
Fax: (773) 761-2957
Pager: (773) 562-7779
Custom metal work

Historic Lighting
114 E. Lemon
Monrovia, CA 91606
(818) 303-4899

Inlight Art Glass
565 Elmwood Ave.
Buffalo, NY 14222
(716) 881-3564

James Ipekjian
768 Fair Oaks Ave.
Pasadena, CA 91103
(818) 792-5025
Specializing in the work
of the Greene Brothers.

Metro Lighting & Crafts
Lawrence Grown
2216 San Peblo Ave.
Berkeley, CA 94702
(510) 540-0509
Fax (510) 540-0549

Mica Lamp Company
520 State St.
Glendale, CA 91203
(818) 241-727
Fax: (818) 240-1074

Mission Spirit
9900 West Spirit Lake Road
Spirit Lake, ID 83869
(800) 433-4211
Fax (208) 623-4865

Roycroft Associates
Design Studio & Gallery
31 S. Grove St.
East Aurora, NY 14052
(716) 652-3333
Fax: (716) 655-0562

Oakbrook-Esser Studios
129 E. Wisconson Ave.
Oconomowoc, WI 53066
(414) 567-9310
Fine Reproductions of the
Frank Lloyd Wright and other
Prairie School designs in
stained and leaded glass

Omega Too
2204 San Pablo
Berkeley, CA 94702
(510) 843-3636

Original Cast Lighting
6120 Delmar Blvd.
St. Louis, MO 63112
(314) 863-1895

Porcelli Studio
64 Woodstock Dr.
Newtown, PA 18940
(215) 860-9947
Reproductions of the work for
Louis Comfort Tiffany

Rejuvenation Lamp and
Fixture Company
1100 SE Grand Ave.
Portland, OR 97214
(503) 231-1900

Rockscapes, Inc.
419 N. Larchmont Blvd., #68
Los Angeles, CA 90068
(800) 469-3637

St. Louis Antique Lighting Co.
801 N. Skinker Blvd.
St. Louis, MO 63130-4844
(314) 863-1414

Dale Tiffany, Inc.
12866 Ann Street
Santa Fe Springs, CA 90670
(310) 903-4500

Auction Houses

Arts & Crafts in Chicago
818 North Blvd.
Oak Park, IL 60302
John Toomey,
Don Treadway
(312) 383-5234
(2) May/October

Butterfield & Butterfield
7601 Sunset Blvd.
Los Angeles, CA 90046
(213) 850-7500
220 San Bruno Avenue
San Francisco, CA 94103
(415) 861-7500 ext. 218

Christies (and Christies East)
502 Park Avenue
New York, NY 10022
Nancy A. McClelland;
(212) 546-1086
(2+) June/December
Craftsman Auctions
(800) 448-7828

Dennis Freeman Interests
7500 Hamilton Ave.
Cincinnati, OH 45231
(513) 931-3222

Philips, New York
406 East 79th Street
New York, NY 10021
Andrew Shapiro,
Susan Pennington
(212) 570-4830
(2) June/December

David Rago Arts & Crafts
Auctions
17 S. Main St.
Lambertville, NJ 08530
(609) 397-9374
(2) Spring & Fall

Savoia's Auction Services
Route 23
South Cairo, NY 12484
Richard Savioia (518) 622-8000
(3-4) January/May/October

Skinner, Inc.
357 Main St.
Bolton, MA 01740
Louise Luther
Garrett Sheehan
(508) 779-6241
(3) January/May/October

Smith & Jones, Inc.
12 Clark Lane
Sudbury, MA 01776
(508) 443-5117
Fax (508) 443-8045

Sotheby's, NY
1334 York Ave. (at 72nd St.)
New York, NY 10021

Treadway Gallery Inc.
2029 Madison Road
Cincinnati, OH 45208
(513) 321-6474

Textiles/Wall & Floor Coverings

AA Abbington Affiliates,Inc.
Tin Ceilings and Walls
2149 Utica Ave.
Brooklyn, NY 11234
(718) 258-8333

Arts & Crafts Period Textiles
Dianne Ayres
5427 Telegraph Ave. W2
Oakland, CA 94609
(510) 654-1645
Pillows, curtains, runners,
bedspreads, embroidery kits,
yardage.

Blue Hill Cooperative
Nancy B. Thomas
22 E. Lanneau Dr.
Greenville, SC 29605
(803) 232-4217
Custom A&C inspired wool
rugs, printed textiles. Custom
orders.

Y.B. Bolour
920 North LaCienega Blvd.
Los Angeles, CA 90069
Rugs and carpets from the
A&C period including Morris
and CFA Voysey, originals.

Bradbury & Bradbury
Wallpaper
P.O Box 155
Benicia, CA 94510
(707) 746-1900

Terry Buck
2 Fairview Avenue
Chatham, NY 12037
Woven fabric

J.R. Burrows & Co.
P.O. Box 522
393 Union Street
Rockland, MA 02370
(800) 347-1795
Fax (617) 982-1636
merchant @ burrows.com;
http://www.burrows.com
Floorcoverings: Suppliers
of William Morris and
C.F.A. Voysey

Carter & Co./Mt. Diablo
Handprints
451 Ryder St.
Vallejo, CA 94590
(707) 745-3388

Country Cottage and Arts
and Crafts Stencils
P.O. Box 10214, Dept. 760025
Des Moines, IA 50336
(800) 678-5681

Dualoy, Inc.
Bill Feigin, leather hides
45 W. 34th St.
New York, NY 10001
(212) 736-3360
Leather, much in the color
and styles of original A & C
material

Helen Foster Stencils
71 Main St.
Sanford, ME 04073
(207) 490-2625
Pre-cut stencils & supplies for
the Arts & Crafts interior

Gordon Galloway
leatherworker
72 Castlewood Drive
Cheektowaga, NY 14227
(716) 668-1742

Jax Rugs
Del Martin
109 Parkway
Berea, KY 40403
(606) 986-5410
Arts & Crafts rugs

Linens by Liza
Liza Jennings Seiner
108 Summerhill Lane
Level Green, PA 15085
(412) 856-8234
Linens for the home, including
counted cross-stitch sampler
kits, pillow kits, placemats,
and table runners

Carol Mead
Borders and Friezes
434 Deerfield Rd.
Pomfret, CT 06259
(860) 963-1927

Nature's Loom
Mark Haroonian
32 East 31st Street
New York, NY 1016
(800) 365-2002;
Fax: (212) 365-2002

Diane Olthius
The Craftsman Style Catalogue
Box 41, Hope, Alaska 99605
(907) 782-3115
All A&C designs, especially
Scandinavian motifs

Persian Carpet
5634 Chapel Hill Blvd.
Durham, NC 27707
(919) 489-8362
Fax (919) 493-3529

Pi-Wy-ACK Studio
Pinson and Ware
P.O. Box 292
Monrovia, CA 91017
(818) 359-6113
A&C Borders and Friezes, hand-
painted and ready to hang

Roycroft Shops
31 S. Grove St.
East Aurora, NY 14052
(716) 655-0562
Leather and linen mats, linen
and cotton runners, pillow
covers, textile kits and
finished goods.

Charles Rupert
2004 Oak Bay Ave.
Victoria, BC V8R 1E4 Canada
(250) 592-4916

Arthur Sanderson and Sons
979 Third Ave.
New York, NY 10022
Original William Morris
designs, block-printed
textiles made in England;
hand-blocked wallpapers
designed by Morris. *To the
trade only.*

San Francisco Victoriana
2070 Newcomb Ave.
San Francisco, CA 94124
(415) 648-0313
Mail-order company,
embossed, die-cut borders.

F. Schumacher and Co.
939 Third Ave.
New York, NY 10022
(212) 415-3909
Frank Lloyd Wright textiles
and custom carpets, various
patterns. *To the trade only.*

Robert Schweitzer
Historic Paint Consulting
3661 Waldenwood
Ann Arbor, MI 48105
(313) 668-0298
Residential, commercial,
museums.

Textile Artifacts
(antique linens)
Paul Freeman
1847 Fifth St.
Manhattan Beach, CA 90267
(310) 379-0207

Richard E. Thibaut, Inc.
480 Frelinghuysen Ave.
Newark, NJ 07114
(201) 643-1118

United Crafts
127 W Putnam Ave.,
Suite 123
Greenwich, CT 06830
(203) 869-4898

Victorian Collectibles Ltd.
845 E. Glenbrook Rd.
Milwaukee, WI 53217
(414) 352-6971
Mail order hand-printed with
and 20th century papers

Ann Wallace and Friends
Textiles For The Home
767 Linwood Ave.
St. Paul, MN 55105
(612) 228-9611

Artwork

Tom Bojanowski, paintings
P.O. Box 436
East Aurora, NY 14052
(716) 652-9353

Dard Hunter Studios
P.O. Box 771
Chillicothe, OH 45601
(614) 774-1236
Wide selection of decorative
items based on Dard Hunter
graphics. (artwork, stationery,
guest books, miscellany)

Inlight Art Glass
Patricia & Guilliano Deganis
565 Elmwood Avenue
Buffalo, NY 14222
(716) 881-3564

Dorothy Markert
Silk Screen Prints
253 Maple Ave.
Hamburg, NY 14075
(716) 649-4052

Anita Munman Design, Inc.
729 S. Carpenter Ave.
Oak Park, IL 60304-1106
(708) 383-2884

Screen Scenes
Warren Coulter
795 Lee Road,
P.O. Box 3625
Quincy, CA 95971
(916) 283-4366

Brian Stewart
Plein Air Paintings &
Woodblock Prints
5321 Xerxes
Minneapolis, MN 55410
(612) 920-4653

Kathleen West
Printmaker
P.O. Box 545, 159 Maple St.
East Aurora, NY 14052
(716) 652-9125

Laura Wilder
Period style prints & portraits
1210 Stockbridge Road
Webster, NY 14580
(716) 872-4318

Hardware

Architectural Products
P.O. Box 347
52 Passaic St.
Wood Ridge, NJ 07075
(800) 835-4400

Arts & Crafts Hardware
Gerry Rucks, Craftsman
Bruce Szopo, Distributor
3860 Ellamae
Oakland, MI 48363
(313) 652-7652

Ball & Ball
Hardware Reproductions
467 W Lincoln Hwy.
Exton, PA 19341
(800) 257-3711

Conant Custom Brass
270 Pine Street
Burlington, VT 05401
(802) 658-4482

Craftsman Hardware Co.
Chris Efker
P.O. Box 161
Marceline, MO 64658
(816) 376-2481
Fax (816) 376-4076

Crown City Hardware Co.
1047 N Allen Ave.
Pasadena, CA 91104
(818) 794-1188

The Decorators Supply
Corporation
Replicas of Hand-carvings
3610 South Morgan
Chicago, IL 60609

Designer's Warehouse
Restoration Works, Fixtures
& Hardware
P.O. Box 486
Buffalo, NY 14205
(716) 856-6400

Eugenia's Antique Hardware
Lance Dobson
5370 Peachtree Road
Chamblee, GA 30341
(770) 458-1677
Fax (770) 458-5966

Hardware Restoration
Ed Donaldson
P.O. Box 38, Dept. D
Boiling Springs, PA 17077
(717) 249-3624

Liz's Antique Hardware
453 S. LaBrea Ave.
Los Angeles, CA 90036
(213) 939-4403

Accessories

Arvid's Woods
Mouldings and Accessories
2820 Rucker Ave.
Everett, WA 98201
(800) 627-8437.

The Aurora Silversmith
Alburn R. Sleeper
P.O. Box 140
East Aurora, NY 14052
(716) 652-6043
Email: asleep220@aol.com
Specializing in Roycroft jewelry
and metal accessories

Dennis Bertucci
A&C mantel clocks
Rd. 3 P.O. Box 451
Walton, NY 13856
(607) 865-8372

Tom Bojanowski, Frames
P.O. Box 436
East Aurora, N.Y. 14052
(716) 652-9363

The Decorators Supply
Corporation
Replicas of Hand-carvings
3610 South Morgan
Chicago, IL 60609
(312) 847-6300

Designer's Warehouse
Restoration Works
P.O. Box 486
Buffalo, NY 14205
(716) 856-6400

Fair Oak Workshops
Custom Restoration
P.O. Box 5578
River Forest, IL 60305
(800) 341-0597

Fine Lines
Framing
P.O. Box 1415
Maplewood, NJ 07040
(201) 763-2349

Susan Hebert
Copper items
2018 NW Irving St.
Portland, OR 97209
(503) 248-1111

Historical Arts Castings, Inc.
Replicated FLW Metalwork
5580 West Bagley Park Rd.
West Jordan, Utah 84088

Holton Furniture and Frame
5515 Doyle Street, Suite 2
Emeryville, CA 94608
(510) 450-0350

Industry Road Gallery
Reproduction Metal Pieces
P.O. Box 771
Cotuit, MA 02635
(508) 428-8623

Omega Too
2204 San Pablo Ave.
Berkeley, CA 94702
(510) 843-3636

Rockscapes
Craftsman Mailboxes
419 N. Larchmont Blvd. #68
Los Angeles, CA 90068

Steptoe and Wife, Ltd.
322 Geary Ave.
Toronto, Canada M6H 2C7
(416) 530-4200

Weidner Workshop
1306 Plymouth Ave.
San Francisco, CA 94112
(415) 587-0374

Pottery & Tiles

Alchemie Ceramics Studio
1550 Gascony Rd.
Leucadia, CA 92024
(619) 942-6051

American Olean Tile Co.
P.O. Box 271
1000 Cannon Ave.
Lansdale, PA 19446
(215) 855-1111

Artesanos
Drawer G
Sante Fe, NM 87504
(505) 983-5563

Bertin Studio Tiles
11 Munson St.
Port Washington, NY 11050
(516) 767-7308

C&C Brown Potters
(541) 336-3668

Shep Brown Associates, Inc.
24 Cummings Park
Woburn, MA 01801
(617) 935-8080

Dedham and Chelsea
Keramic Pottery, Jim Kaufman
248 Highland Street
Dedham, MA 02026
(800) 283-8070
(617) 329-8070
Fax: (617) 329-9538

Deer Creek Pottery
305 Richardson St.
Grass Valley, CA 95945
(916) 272-3373

Designs in Tile
Selene Seltzer
Box 358, Dept. CHO
Mount Shasta, CA 96067
(916) 926-2629
Fax (916) 926-6467
www.designsintile.com

Dropped Shop
Museum quality restoration
of Art Pottery
21 Elm Street
East Aurora, NY 14052
(716) 652-7053

Dy's Art Tiles
1136 Nittany Crest Ave.
Bellefonte, PA 16823
(814) 383-2011

Ephraim Faience Pottery
P.O. Box 792
Brookfield, WI 53008-0792
(888) 704-7687

Epro, Inc.
156 E. Broadway
Westerville, OH 43801
(614) 882-6990

Fulper Tile
P.O. Box 373
Yardley, PA 19067
(215) 736-8512

H & R Johnson Tiles
P.O. Box 2335
Farmingdale, NJ 07727
(908) 280-7900

Handcraft Tile
1696 S. Main St.
Milpitas, CA 95035
(408) 262-1140

K.J. Patterson Ceramics
590 Ayon Avenue
Azusa, CA 91702
(818) 815-2695

The Moravian-Mercer
Pottery & Tile Works/
Fonthill Museum
130 Swamp Road
Doylestown, PA 18901
(215) 345-6722 / 348-9461

Motawi Tileworks
33 N. Staebler Ste. 2
Ann Arbor, MI 48103
(313) 213-0017

Old World Restorations Inc.
347 Stanley Ave.
Cincinnati, OH 45226
(513) 321-1911

Pewabic Pottery & Tile Works
10125 E. Jefferson
Detroit, MI 48214
(313) 822-0954
Web: www.pewabic.com

Rookwood Pottery Co.
4515 Page Avenue
Michigan Center, MI 49254
(517) 764-5585

The Roycroft Potters
Janice McDuffie
37 South Grove St.
East Aurora, NY 14052
(716) 652-7422

Charles Rupert Designs
2004 Oak Bay Ave.
Victoria, BC V8R 1E4 Canada
(604) 592-4916

Malvena Solomon, Inc.
1122 Madison Ave.
New York, NY 10025
(212) 535-5200
Wide selection of period
art pottery.

Starbuck Goldner Tiles
315 W. Fourth St.
Bethlehem, PA 18015
(610) 866-6321

Sun House Tiles
9986 Happy Acres W.
Bozeman, MT 59715
(406) 587-3651 / 587-1175

Tile Restoration Center
3511 Interlake N.
Seattle, WA 98103
(206) 633-4866

Tile Showcase
Boston Design Center,
Suite 639
Boston, MA
(617) 426-6515

Van Briggle Art Pottery
P.O. Box 96
Colorado Springs, CO 80901
(719) 633-4080

Venice Tile Collections
24425 Woolsey Canyon Rd.
#12
West Hills, CA 91304

Jerome Venneman Pottery
658-66th St.
Oakland, CA
(510) 653-5106

Winters Tileworks
Diane Winters
2547 8th Street, #33
Berkeley, CA 94710
(510) 533-7624

Furnishings

American Arts & Crafts Co.
Custom designs.
Ben C. Toledano
P.O. Box 3140
Covington, LA 70434
(504) 893-9962

American Furnishings Co.
1423A Grandview Ave.
Columbus, OH 43212
(614) 488-7263
Fax: (614) 488-7264

Arroyo Design
Custom designed furniture.
244 North 4th Ave.
Tucson, AZ 85705
Attn: Elaine Paul
(602) 884-1012

V. Michael Ashford
Craftsman inspired designs
in copper and oak.
6543 Alpine Dr. S.W.
Olympia, WA 98512
(360) 352-0694

W.D. Bosworth
Woodworking
1108 Charles St.
Beaufort, SC 29902
(803) 522-3942
Fax: (803) 522-3057

Todd Brotherton
P.O. Box 404
Mt. Shasta, CA 96067
(916) 938-4000 vox/fax
toddb@compuserve.com
H. Ellis and Greene & Greene
are his specialty.

Cathers & Dembrosky
43 East 10th Street
New York, NY 10003
(212) 353-1244
Specialize in fine A&C, furniture, metalwork, lighting and accessories

Coppertree Woodworks
2248 Shillelagh Rd.
Chesapeake, VA 23323
(804) 421-7328

Craftsman Collection
2551 Regency Rd.,
Suite 188
Lexington, KY 40503
(606) 277-7500

The Craftsman
Ron Cosser & Lyle Noreault
110 Walter Drive
Eastwood, NY 13206
(315) 463-0262

The Craftsman Home
3048 Claremont Ave.
Berkeley, CA 94705
(510) 655-6503
Fax: (510) 655-5501

Craftsman Home Resource Ctr.
50 Bull Hill Road
Wood Stoke, CT 06281
(860) 928-6662

Custom Woodcrafters
P.O. Box 391
Budd Lake, NJ 07828
(800) 455-7585
Fax: (908) 852-7468

DenCraft
P.O. Box 9478
Naples, FL 33941
(941) 352-1615
Fax: (941) 352-6728

Arnold d'Epagnier
14201 Notley Rd.
Colesville, MD 20904
(301) 384-1663

Geoffrey Fitzwilliam, Co.
2109 W. 2200 South
Salt Lake City, UT 84119
(810) 974-5977
Fax: (810) 596-8933

Michael Flaxman
Woodworking: Custom
inspired furnishings in the
Arts & Crafts style
34 Auburn Ave.
Jamestown, NY 14701
(716) 484-0551

Green Design Furniture
267 Commercial Street
Portland, ME 04101
(207) 775-4234
Solid cherry furniture

Thomas Gardner Woodcraft
2594 East Walnut St.
Pasadena, CA 91103
(818) 449-2594

The Hammersmith Collection
P.O. Box 317
Buffalo, NY 14213
(800) 884-5930
Fax: (716) 884-5930

Heart & Hand Furniture
1508 7th Ave.
Waterlivet, NY 12189
(518) 270-0860

Warren Hile Studio
89 E. Montecito Ave.
Sierra Madre, CA 91024
(818) 355-4382
Fax: (818) 355-7705

Holton Furniture & Frame
5515 Doyle St. #2
Emeryville, CA 94608
(510) 450-0350

George Hunter Designs
Contract craftsman.
Greene & Greene designs
faithfully reproduced.
21877 Eighth St. East; P.O.
Box 841, Sonoma, CA 95476
(707) 938-4552

James-Randell
Reproductions of interior
designs of Greene & Greene.
Jim Ipekjian,
768 Fair Oaks Ave.
Pasadena, CA 91103
(818) 792-5025

Paul Kemner
2829 Rockwood
Toledo, OH 43610
(419) 241-8278
pkemner@bright.net

Kevin Kopil Furniture Design
P.O. Box 411, Route 2
Jonesville, VT 05466
(802) 434-4400
Fax: (802) 434-5639

Lower's Furniture
& Cabinetry
Bill & Chris Lower
425 Floral Ave.
Ithaca, NY 14850
(607) 277-4769
Original and contemporary
mission furniture and
accessories.

Mack & Rodell
44 Leighton Rd.
Pownal, ME 04069
(207) 688-4483
http://www.neaguild.com/mac
rodel
Original interpretations of
Mackintosh, Voysey, Harvey
Ellis and others.

"Homeworks"
P.O. Box 334
Pittsfield, ME 04967
Phone/Fax: (207) 948-5330

Mission Possible
New Craftsman Furnishings
5516 Connecticut Ave, NW
Washington, D.C. 20015
(202) 363-6897

Mission Woodworks
100 Zorana Pl.
San Pedro, CA 90732
Phone/Fax: (310) 519-7966

Old Hickory Furniture Co., Inc.
403 S. Noble St.
Shelbyville, IN 46176
(800) 232-BARK
Fax: (317) 398-2275

Darrell Peart Furnituremaker
625 Western Ave.
Seattle, WA 98104
(206) 935-2874

M. Puhalski Furniture &
Design, Inc.
3400 13th Ave. SW
Seattle, WA 98134
(206) 233-9581
(888) 590-1952 (toll-free)

Prairie Woodworking
343 Harrison St.
Oak Park, IL 60304
Phone/Fax (708) 386-0603

The Roycroft Shops
31 South Grove St.
East Aurono, NY 14052
(716) 652-3333
Fax: (716) 655-0562
Email: rycrft@aol.com
All aspects of A&C
reproductions

The Schoolhouse Gallery
Tom Harris & Ben Little
1054 Olean Road
East Aurora, NY 14052
(716) 655-4080

Signature Cabinets
Neil Kelly
801 N. Alberta
Portland, OR 97217
(503) 288-7461

Silverfish Design
1110 Stearns Hill Rd.
Waltham, MA 02154
(617) 894-3076

Solid Cedar Design
P.O. Box 1044
Newark, DE 19715-1044
(302) 737-9987

Swartzendruber Hardwood
Creations
1100 Chicago Ave.
Goshen, IN 46526
(800) 531-2502
Fax: (219) 534-2504

Tillman Studios
9 Fairview Ave.
Chatham, NY 12037
(518) 392-4603

True To Form
73 Manchester St.
San Francisco, CA 94110
(415) 864-0111

Vulpiani Workshop Inc.
Custom finishings of
Stickley re-issues.
Coly Vulpiani
5446 Route 212
Mount Trempe, NY 12457
(914) 688-2585

Water Valley Woodwork
3714 South Hill Rd.
Hamburg, NY 14075
(716) 649-6032

Debey Zito
55 Bronte St.
San Francisco, CA 94111
(415) 648-6861

Commercial Companies Making Arts & Crafts Style Furniture

Atelier International
Mackintosh Reproductions
30-20 Thomson Ave.
Long Island City, NY 11101
(212) 223-7449

Baker Furniture
Casegoods/Upholstery
1661 Monroe Ave. NW
Grand Rapids, MI 49505
(616) 361-7321

Bassett Furniture
Complete line of casegoods
and upholstery furniture
P.O. Box 626
Bassett, VA 24055
(703) 629-6000

Crownpoint Cabinetry
P.O. Box 1560
153 Charlestown Rd.
Claremont, NH 03743
(800) 999-4994

Ethan Allen
American Impressions-a blend
of Mission and Shaker (See
local phone directory-hundreds
of dealers nationwide)

The Kennebec Company
One Front St.
Bath, ME 04530
(207) 443-2131

Lane Furniture
Grove Park Collection
East Franklin Ave.
Alta Vista, VA 24517
(804) 369-5641

The Michaels Company
5849 88th St.
Sacramento, CA 95828
(916) 381-9086

National Mt. Airy Furniture
The "new" Pasadena Line
P.O. Box 669
Bassett, VA 24055
(703) 629-2501

Richardson Brothers Company
Dining room furniture
P.O. Box 907
Sheboygan Falls, WI 53085
(414) 467-4631

Romweber Furniture Co.
A&C Oak entertainment
center only
Four S. Park Ave.
Batesville, IN 47006
(812) 934-3485

Stanley Furniture
Urban Primitives line by
Robert Sonnemann
P.O. Box 30
Stanleytown, VA 24168
(703) 629-7561

L&JG Stickley Company
Cherry and mission oak collection, Roycroft Reproductions
Stickley Dr./ P.O. Box 480
Manlius, NY 13104
(315) 682-5500

Taylor Woodcraft, Inc.
Dining, chairs, stools, bedroom
P.O. Box 245
South River Rd.
Malta, OH 43758
(614) 962-3741

Geoffrey D. Warner
Fine Furniture and Cabinetry
99 Pardon Joslin Rd.
Exeter, RI 02822
(401) 295-1243

Woodmode
Fine Custom Cabinetry
One 2nd St.
Kreamer, PA 17833
(717) 374-2711

Arts & Crafts Museum Houses & Collections
See also Wright sites.

NORTHEAST

Buffalo & Erie County
Library Rare Book Room
Lafayette Square
Buffalo, NY 14203

Burchfield-Penney Art Center
1300 Elmwood Ave.
Buffalo, NY 14222
(716) 878-6011

Carnegie Museum of Arts
4400 Forbes Ave.
Pittsburgh, PA 15213
(412) 622-3320

Chautauqua Institute
Chautauqua, NY
(716) 357-6200

Craftsman Farms/Gustav
Stickley
2352 Rt. 10W.
Parsippany, NJ 07950
(201) 540-1165

Everson Museum
Syracuse, NY
(315) 474-6064

Fonthill Museum
E. Court St.
Doylestown, PA 18901
(215) 348-9461

Alexis Jean Fournier House*
East Aurora, NY 14052
(thru Roycroft Shops)
(716) 652-3333
By appointment only.

Elbert Hubbard Museum
ScheideMantle House
363 Oakwood Ave.
E. Aurora, NY 14052
(716) 652-4735
(Open June-Oct.)

Mercer Museum
84 S. Pine
Doylestown, PA 18901
(215) 345-0210

Metropolitan Museum of Art
Fifth Avenue
New York, NY

Moravian Pottery &
Tile Works
130 Swamp Rd. (Rt 313)
Doylestown, PA 18901
(215) 348-9461

Museum of Fine Arts
465 Huntington Ave.
Boston, MA 02115
(617) 2647-9300

Newark Museum-Newark, NJ
(201) 596-5386

Rockwell Museum-Corning, NY
(607) 937-5386

Roycroft Campus
South Grove St., E. Aurora, NY
Roycroft Inn (716) 652-5552
Roycroft Shops (716) 652-3333
Open 7 Days a week

Rush-Rhees Library
Rare Book Collection
University of Rochester
Rochester, NY 14627
(716) 275-3302

Strong Museum
One Manhattan Sq.
Rochester, NY 14607
(716) 275-3302

Winterthur Library
Winterthur, DE 19735
(302) 654-1548
(800) 448-3883

MIDWEST

Chicago Institute of Art,
Chicago, IL
(312) 443-3600

Cincinnati Art Museum,
Cincinnati, OH
(513) 721-5204

Cranbrook House/Academy
of Art Museum
500 Lone Pine Rd.
Bloomfield Hills, MI 48103
(313) 645-3300

The Detroit Institute of Art
5200 Woodward Ave.
Detroit, MI 48202
(313) 833-7900

Glessner House
1800 S. Prairie Ave.
Chicago, IL 60616
(312) 326-1480

Palmer College of Chiropractic
1000 Brady St.
Davenport, IA 52803
(319) 326-9600
By appointment only

Purcell-Cuts House
2328 Lake Place
Minneapolis, MN
870-3131 (Open 2nd Sat.
of each month, 10-5)

SOUTH

High Museum of Art
1280 Peachtree St. N.E.
Atlanta, GA 30309
(404) 892-3600

Virginia Museum of Art
Richmond, VA
(804) 367-0852

SOUTHWEST

D.M. Francis House*
1456 West Meade Lane
Flagstaff, AZ 86001
"Plateau Winds"
call (602) 773-1284

Northern Arizona University-
Rare Book Collection
Library-Flagstaff, AZ
(602) 523-2171 / 523-9011

The Riordan House
Riordan Park
State of Arizona Historic Site
Flagstaff, AZ
(602) 779-4395

WEST

Boettcher Mansion
Susan Becker, Director
900 Colorow Road
Golden, CO 80401
(303) 526-0855
cain@co.jefferson.co.us*http://
co.jefferson.co.us/mansion.htm
A 1917 Arts & Crafts Estate
in the Colorado Rockies for
conferences, weddings,
special events.

Buffalo Bill Museum
720 Sheridan Ave.
Cody, WY 82414
(307) 587-4771

Bungalow Heaven
Neighborhood Assoc.
P.O. Box 40672
Pasadena, CA 91104
(Tours Annually)*

The Gamble House
4 Westmoreland Pl.
Pasadena, CA 91103-3593
(818) 793-3334
(213) 681-6427

Grace Hudson Museum
Sun House
431 S. Main St.
Ukiah, CA 95482
(707) 462-3370

Huntington Library
1151 Oxford Road
San Marino, CA 91108
(626) 405-2141

Los Angeles County
Museum of Art
5905 Wilshire Blvd.
Los Angeles, CA 90036
(213) 857-6000

The Martson House
3525 Seventh Ave.
San Diego, CA 92138
(619) 298-3142

Oakland Museum of Art
Oak & 10th St.
Oakland, CA 94618
(510) 238-3401

University of Texas
(Rare Book Room)

*Require appointments - some are
now private homes. All museums
have varying schedules which
should be checked.

The Wright Sites

*The following sites offer
guided tours. It is suggested
that you call ahead to confirm
dates, times and fees.*

Dana-Thomas House -
Guided tours of the recently
restored Springfield, Ill.,
house are offered daily from
9 a.m.-5 p.m. at 301 E.
Lawrence Ave., Springfield,
IL 62706. Tickets, which are
free, can be reserved for a
specific date and time by
calling (217) 782-6776.
CHO member.

Ennis-Brown House -
Guided tours by reservation
only. Second Saturday of
every odd numbered month.
(Jan., March, May, etc.)
Reserve by sending $10 each
adult, $5 for student and senior
citizens, to Ennis-Brown
House; 2655 Glendower Ave.;
Los Angeles, CA 90027.
Phone (213) 660-0607.

Fallingwater - Weekend,
guided tours, mid-November-
March. Daily tours, mid-mid
Nov. (Closed Mondays) 10
a.m.-4 p.m. $6 weekdays, $8
weekends. Two hour, in-depth
tour offered at 9 a.m. on regular tour days. $20 per person.
Reservations required for all
tours. Fallingwater; P.O. Box
R; Mill Run, PA 15464.
Call (412) 329-8501.

**Frank Lloyd Wright Home
& Studio** - Guided tours of
Wright's Oak Park residence
and workplace. Mon.-Fri., 11
a.m., 1 & 3 p.m.; Sat. & Sun.,
11 a.m.-4 p.m. $5 adults, $3
senior and youths 10-18. Free
to children under 10. 651
Chicago Ave., Oak Park, IL
60302. Phone (708) 848-1500.
CHO member.

**Grady Gammage Memorial
Auditorium** - Half-hour guid-
ed tours Mon.-Sat., 1:30-3:30
p.m. Free. Arizona State
University campus at
Gammage Parkway and
Apache Blvd., Tempe, AZ
85287. Call (602) 965-3434.

Hillside Home School -
Guided tours of the buildings
Wright designed for his aunts
Jane and Nell Lloyd Jones and
later adapted for the Taliesin
Fellowship. April 19-Oct.
Seven days a week, 9 a.m.-
4 p.m. $6 adults, $3 children,
5-12. Highway 23, Spring
Green, WI 53588. Phone (608)
588-2511.

Hollyhock House - Guided
tours: Tues., Wed. & Thurs.;
10 a.m., 11, noon & 1 p.m.
Every Sat. at 1, 2 & 3 p.m.
First, second and third Sunday
of each month at 1, 2 & 3
p.m. $1.50 adults, $1 seniors.
4800 Hollyhock Blvd., Los
Angeles, CA 90027. Call (213)
662-7272.

**Johnson Wax
Administration Building** -
Guided tours: Tues.-Fri; 9:45
a.m., 11:30, 1 p.m. & 2:45.
(Closed Mon., weekends &
holidays.) Free. Reservations
recommended. 1525 Howe St.,
Racine, WI 53403. Phone
(414) 631-2154.

Kentuck Knob - P.O. Box
305, Chalk Hill, PA 15421,
(412) 329-1901. Tuesday-
Sunday: 10-4 pm. $10 week-
days; $15 Weekends.
Reservations recommended.

Marin County Civic Center -
Tours of Wright's government
building are offered by
appointment. 3501 Civic
Center Dr., San Rafael, CA
94903. Call (415) 499-7407.

Meyer May House - Tours:
Tues. & Thurs., 10 a.m.-2
p.m.; Sundays, 1-5 p.m. Free
(Closed some days). 450
Madison St.. SE, Grand Rapids,
MI 49503. Phone (616) 246-
4821.

Pope-Leighy House - Guided
tours daily: March-Dec.
Weekend tours: Jan. & Feb.
9:30 a.m.-4:30 p.m. $4 adults,
$3 seniors & students through
highschool. Children under 5
free. Located three miles south
of Mt. Vernon at 9000
Richmond Hwy., Alexandria,
VA 22309. Call (703) 780-3264.

Price Tower - Tours of this
19-story highrise built for H.C.
Price in 1956 are offered
Thurs., 1 p.m., 1:30 & 2 or by
appointment. Donations are
requested. 6th & Dewey St.,
Bartlesville, OK. Write:
Landmark Society, P.O. Box
941, Bartlesville, OK 74005.

Robie House - Guided tours
of Wright's 1908 house for
Frederick C. Robie, now part
of the University of Chicago
campus. Seven days a week
at noon. $2 adults, $1 students
& seniors. Free for children
under 10. 5757 Woodlawn
Ave., Chicago, IL 60637.
Phone (312) 702-8374.

**Stanley & Mildred
Rosenbaum House** - Guided
tours by reservation only of
this 1939-40 Usonian House.
Tours daily: 10 a.m.-5 p.m.
$5 for individuals, $4 groups
of four or more, seniors
& students. Call or write:
The Risenbaum House, 601
Riverview Dr., Florence, AL
35630. Call (205) 764-5274.

Taliesin Walking Tour -
Guided, 1½ hr. walking tour of
the Taliesin property. Departs
from Hillside School. Mid-June
to Sept., Mon.-Sat., 10:30 a.m.
$15 per person. Spring Green,
WI 53588. Phone (608) 588-
2511.

Taliesin West - Two types of
guided tours now available.
1 hr. guided tour: Mon.-
Thurs., 1-4 p.m.; Fri-Sun., 9
a.m.-4 p.m. on the hour. $10
(Summers, June-Sept, daily,
8 a.m.-11 on the hour. $6)
"Behind the Scenes" - an
exclusive, in-depth tour featuring the Taliesin West living &
dining rooms, refreshments &
and desert walk. Call for exact
times. Cactus Road & 108th
St., Scottsdale, AZ 85261. Call
(602) 860-2700.

Wingspread - The home
Wright designed in 1937 for
Herbert F. Johnson of the
Johnson Wax Co. Opens only
when conferences are not in
session. 33 E. Four Mile Rd.,
Wind Point, WI. Phone (414)
639-3211.

Unity Temple - Tape recorded
tour offered Mon.-Fri., 2 p.m.-
4. $4 adults, $2 seniors &
students. Custom tours for
groups by reservation. 875
Lake St., Oak Park, IL 60301.
Call (708) 848-6225.

Zimmerman House -
Guided tours of the Isadore J.
& Lucille Zimmerman House
are scheduled Thurs., Fri. &
Sat., 10 a.m.-3 p.m. and Sun.,
1 p.m.-3:30; $4 adults, $2.50
students & seniors. Tours
depart from the Currier
Gallery of Art, 192 Orange St.,
Manchester, NH 03104.
Reservations are strongly
recommended.
Phone (603) 626-4158.

Bookstores

Builder's Booksource
1 (800) 843-2028

Frank Lloyd Wright Home &
Studio
951 Chicago Ave.
Oak Park, IL 60302
(708) 848-1976

The Gamble House Bookstore
4 Westmoreland Pl.
Pasadena, CA 91103
(818) 449-4178
Fax: (818) 405-0466

Linden Publishing
Specialist Bookseller &
Publisher
336 W. Bedford, Ste. 107
Fresno, CA 93726
(209) 227-2901
Fax: (209) 227-3520
Send for free catalog of over
300 books & videos on all
fields of woodworking.

Roycroft Shops
31 S. Grove Street
East Aurora, NY 14052
(716) 655-0571
Fax: (716) 655-0562

RUBBER STAMPS
& STATIONERY

Ries Productions
490 Monterico Rd.
Grants Pass, OR 97526

STATIONERY/PRINTS

Mountain House Press
P.O. Box 771
Chillicothe, OH 45601
Based on the designs and
graphics of Dard Hunter
(614) 774-1236

Catalogues, Magazines &
Newsletters

MAGAZINES

American Bungalow John
Brinkman, graphic designer
and Al Griffin, printer. This
publication has proven itself
to be among the most helpful
and attractive of the A&C jour-
nals available. For a subscription, write: P.O. Box 756, 123
South Baldwin Ave.; Sierra
Madre, CA 91025-0756; or call
1 (800) 350-3363.

*Craftsman HomeOwner News-
letter* Official publication of
the Foundation for the Study
of the Arts & Crafts Movement
at Roycroft. More than a
newsletter, it is the most
indepth look at the Arts &
Crafts Movement's history and
Revival: the ideals, the philosophy, the look and the
lifestyle. This journal is nine
years old and each issue is a
focus on one facet of the A/C
Era. Last issue was "Women of
the A/C Period & Today," this
issue is a complete resource
guide. The Autumn/Holiday
issue will be on Ireland, Wales,
(continued)

Isle of Man, and England
(London and the Cotswolds).
Other past issues dealt with
Roycroft, Frank Lloyd Wright,
or Scotland and the British
Isles. The publication is
devoted to the Study of the
International Arts & Crafts
Movement. It is on recycled
paper in 3-ring notebook
format; binders with Charter
Member Cover. Back issues are
avilable ($5.00 each; $150 for
30+ issues).

Home Magazine is also a fine
publication and almost always
includes articles on the Arts
and Crafts style. P.O. Box
10179, Des Moines, IA 50347-
0179. (800) 247-5470.

Old House Journal Beautiful
and informative, this magazine
seems to have a fondness for
Arts and Crafts and related
styles. P.O. Box 56008;
Boulder, CO 80323-6008.
(508) 281-8803.

Style 1900, published by
David Rago, editor in chief, is
the longest on-going treasure
book of scholarly articles.
Formerly (10 years) known as
"Arts and Crafts Quarterly," it
may be found on newsstands
as well as by subscription at
17 South Main Street,
Lambertville, NJ 08530, or call
(609) 397-4104. This publication is a must for any Arts &
Crafts enthusiast.

Old House Interiors is an
excellent magazine and
always features Arts & Crafts
advertisers and interesting
period articles. We recom-
mend this as one of the best.

The Tabby is a letterpress
printed, hand-bound magazine
of ideas issued periodically
throughout the year. A magazine of study, discussion,
analysis, contemplation,
criticism, laughter, thought,
debate, and hope. It is the
work of Bruce Smith and
Yoshiko Yamamoto's Arts &
Crafts Press, P.O. Box 5217,
Berkeley, CA 94705; (510)
849-2117. Already collectible.

Books

GENERAL ARTS AND
CRAFTS

*Alphonse Mucha: His Life &
Art* by Jiri Mucha

*The American Arts and Crafts
Movement in Western New
York* by Bruce Austin

Arts & Crafts (Architecture and
Design Library) by Kitty
Turgeon and Robert Rust

*Arts & Crafts Designs in
America: A State-by-State
Guide* by James Massey and
Shirley Maxwell

The Arts and Crafts Movement
by Adams

The Arts and Crafts Movement
by Elizabeth Cumming and
Wendy Kaplan

The Arts and Crafts Movement
by Gillian Naylor

*The Arts and Crafts Movement
in America, 1876–1916* by
Robert Judson Clark

*The Arts and Crafts Movement
in California: Living the Good
Life* by Kenneth R. Trapp

The Arts and Crafts Price Guide–Metalwork, Lighting, Graphics, and Textiles by Treadway Gallery

Arts and Crafts Style by Isabelle Anscombe

The Art Nouveau Style by Roberta Waddell, ed.

As Bees in Honey Drown: The Loves, Lives & Letters of the Roycroft's Alice and Elbert Hubbard

California Design, 1910 by Andersen, Moore, and Winter

The Book of the Roycrofters: Being a Catalogue of Copper, Leather, and Books by Nancy Hubbard Brady

Charles Rennie Mackintosh by Alan Crawford

Charles Rennie Mackintosh by Wendy Kaplan, ed.

Collector's Style Guide, Arts and Crafts: A New Buyer's Guide to the Decorative Arts, 1880–1931 by Haslam

Drama in Design: The Life and Craft of Charles Rohlfs by Michael L. James

The Encyclopedia of Arts and Crafts: The International Arts Movement by Wendy Kaplan

Gamble House: Greene and Greene by Edward R. Bosley

Glasgow School of Art by James Macauley

Greene & Greene: The Passion and the Legacy by Randell L. Makinson

Greene & Greene Masterworks by Bruce Smith

Gustav Stickley, The Craftsman by Mary Ann Smith

Hill House by James Macauley

The Ideal Home: The History of the Twentieth Century American Craft, 1900–1920, Janet Dardon, editor

Late 19th and 20th Century Decorative Arts by Brandt

Liberty of London, Masters of Style and Decoration by Stephen Calloway

The Life of William Morris by J.W. Mackall

Millers Art Nouveau and Art Deco Buyer's Guide by Eric Knowles, ed.

Nineteenth-Century Design from Pugin to Mackintosh by Charlotte Gere and Michael Whiteway

Official Identification and Price Guide to Arts and Crafts: The Early Modernist Movement in American Decorative Arts, 1891–1923, Second Edition, by Bruce Johnson

Official Price Guide to Arts and Crafts by Bruce Johnson

Part Seen, Part Imagines: Meaning and Symbolism in the Work of Charles Rennie Mackintosh and Margaret MacDonald by Timothy Neat

Rebel with Reverence: Elbert Hubbard—A Granddaughter's Tribute by Mary Roelofs Stott

Treasures of the American Arts and Crafts Movement by Tod Volpe and Beth Cathers

Viennese Design and the Wiener Werkstatte by Kalir

William Morris by Linda Parry, ed.

William Morris: Art and Kelmscott by Linda Parry, ed.

ARCHITECTURE AND LANDSCAPING

The American Bungalow by Clay Lancaster

American Bungalow Style by Robert Winter

Arts & Crafts Architecture by Peter Davey

Arts & Crafts Gardens by Wendy Hitchman

The Bungalow: America's Arts & Crafts Home by Paul Duchscherer & Douglas Keister

California Bungalow by Robert Winter

Craftsman Bungalows by Gustav Stickley

Houses and Gardens: Arts & Crafts Interiors by M.H. Baillie Scott

Inside the Bungalow: America's Arts & Crafts Interiors by Paul Duchscherer and Douglas Keister

Radford's Artistic Bungalows: The Complete 1908 Catalog by Radford Architectural Co.

Toward a Simpler Way of Life: The Arts & Crafts Architects of California by Robert Winter

The Wright Sites by Arlene Anderson

FURNITURE

Arts & Crafts Furniture Design: The Grand Rapids Contribution by Don Marek

The Arts & Crafts Price Guide–Furniture I by Treadway Gallery

The Arts & Crafts Price Guide–Furniture II by Treadway Gallery

Building Arts & Crafts Furniture by Paul Kemner and Peggy Zdila

Furniture of the American Arts & Crafts Movement by David M. Cathers

Furniture of the Arts & Crafts Period: Stickley, Limbert, Mission Oak, Roycroft, Frank Lloyd Wright, and Others by Treadway Galleries

Greene & Greene: Furniture and Related Designs by Randell Makinson

Gustav Stickley: His Craft by Patricia A. Bartinique

Pegged Joint: Restoring Arts & Crafts Furniture and Finishes by Bruce Johnson.

A Rediscovery–Harvye Ellis: Artist, Architect by Jean R. France

Roycroft Furniture, catalog reprint

Roycroft Handmade Furniture by Nancy Hubbard Brady

GLASS

The Collector's Encyclopedia of American Art Glass by Sherman

Frank Lloyd Wright Stained Glass by Thomas A. Heinz

Handel Lamps, Painted Shades, and Glassware by Robert DeFalco

Tiffany's Glass, Bronzes and Lamps by Koch

LIGHTING

The Arts & Crafts Studio of Dirk Van Erp Essay by Lamoureux

Early Twentieth Century Lighting by Sherwood Ltd.

METALS

Archibald Knox by Stephen A. Martin, ed.

Arts and Crafts Metalwork and Silver by Joanna Wissinger and Mark Seelen

A Catalogue of Roycrofters Featuring Metalwork and Lighting Fixtures, introduction by Raymond Groll

Jewelry and Metalwork in the Arts and Crafts Tradition by Elyse Zorn Karlin

Pre-Raphaelite and Arts & Crafts Jewelry by Charlotte Gere and Geoffrey C. Mann

Roycroft Art Metal by Kevin McConnell

Roycroft Collectibles by Charles Hamilton

What is Wrought in the Craftsman Workshops by Gray

POTTERY

American Art Pottery by Vance E. Koehler

American Art Pottery by David Rago

American Art Pottery by Dick Sigafoose

American Art Pottery from the Collection of the Everson Museum of Art by Barbara A. Perry

American Art Tiles by Norman Karlson

American Ceramics, 1876 to the Present, Revised Edition, by Garth Clark

Art Pottery of the United States, Second Edition, by Evans

The Arts and Crafts Price Guide–Ceramics by Treadway Gallery

The Ceramics of William H. Grueby: The Spirit of the New Ideas in Artistic Handicraft by Susan J. Montgomery

Kovel's American Art Pottery: The Collectors Guide to Makers, Marks and Factory Histories by Ralph and Terry Kovel

TEXTILES

Charles Rennie Mackintosh: Textile Designs by Roger Billcliffe.

Craftsman Fabric and Needlework by Gustav Stickley

Textiles of the Arts & Crafts Movement by Linda Parry

William Morris Textiles by Linda Parry

Online Services

Arts & Crafts Society: Marketplace, Carol Kamm, Director of Operations
1209 W. Huron
Ann Arbor, MI 48103
(313) 665-4729
Fax: (313) 213-0045
http://www.arts-crafts.com,
Home of an active online community dedicated to the philosophy and spirit of the original arts & crafts movement.

Web Page of the Roycrofters
Developed by John Petty (FRA-in-charge)
http://www.roycrofter.com/index.shtml
All the information you could ask for about Roycroft! Includes Roycroft Forum, Roycroft Web Shop, and more

Annual Shows
Conferences, Symposiums

Craftsman Farms
2352 Rt. 10
Parsippany, NJ 07950
(201) 540-1165
Third weekend in September

Foundation for the Study of the A&C Movement at Roycroft
31 S. Grove St.
East Aurora, NY 14052
(716) 652-3333
November - second weekend
Annual California Symposium
First week of August

Frank Lloyd Wright Home & Studio Foundation
951 Chicago Ave.
Oak Park, IL 60302
(708) 848-1976
Annual Housewalk - May

Grove Park Inn Conference
Asheville, NC
(800) 438-5800
February - 3rd weekend
Bruce Johnson, Coordinator
(704) 254-1912

Pasadena Heritage
651 S. St. John Ave.
Pasadena, CA 91105
(818) 441-6333
November

Prairie Arts & Crafts Conference
Millikin University (Ed Walker)
1184 W. Main St.
Decatur, IL 62522
(217) 424-6228
September

Roycroft Summer Festival
Roycrofters-at-Large Assn. (RALA), P.O. Box 417
East Aurora, NY 14052
Last weekend of June
Roycroft Winter Festival - First weekend in December.

San Francisco Show & Sale
Concourse Exhibition Center
8th & Brannon Streets
San Francisco, CA
(415) 599-3326 - August

Hotels, Inns, Bed & Breakfasts

Boettcher Mansion - 900 Colorow Road, Golden, Colorado 80401 (303) 526-0855. A 1917 Arts & Crafts Estate in the Colorado Rockies for conferences, weddings, special events.

Cane River House - 910 Washington Street, Natchitoches, LA 71457 (318) 352-5912. Alan and Janny Pezaro: proprietors. Rates: $70 to $95. Visa/Mastercard accepted. Full breakfast is served. Natchitoches, founded in 1714, is the oldest settlement in the Louisiana Purchase and is the home of the Cane River Creole National Park and the National Center for Preservation Technology and Training. The house is in the heart of the historic district, convenient to Plantations and the Kisatchie National Forest. Built in 1923, this craftsman bungalow has a side gabled roof. The interior has original heart pine woodwork, including a floor to ceiling bookcase in the entry. The public rooms are decorated with original arts and crafts furniture, Maxfield Parrish prints, and art pottery; including Van Briggle, Rookwood and Weller. CHO members.

Collins House - Madison, WI (608) 255-4230. Double Occupancy: $85-140 includes full breakfast. A prairie school house.

Cowper Inn - 705 Cowper St., Palo Alto, CA 94301 (415) 327-4475. Rates: $110 per night. Visa/Mastercard accepted. Located near Stanford University and easy access to public transportation to San Francisco and San Jose. Arts & Crafts style house with some very appropriate furnishing. considered a Victorian, the genes are evident. Seasonal breakfast with fresh fruits and baked breads, wine in the afternoon. Each room is furnished with antiques, TV, and telephone.

Craftsman Inn - 7300 East Genesee St., Fayetteville, NY 13066 (315) 637-8000. Rates: $75-$90. Conveniently located near Syracuse, the Craftsman Inn showcases the fine workmanship of L. & J. G. Stickley, Inc. Each room and suite, decorated with either traditional, or Arts & Crafts Stickley furniture, has all the modern comfort amenities. Complimentary continental breakfast .

Gaslight Inn - 1727 15th Ave., Seattle, WA 98122 (206) 325-3654. Innkeepers: Trevor Logan and Stephen Bennett. Rates: $68-$148 depending on room. Conveniently located in the heart of the city, on Seattle's exciting Capitol Hill. Four square built in 1906. Common rooms decorated in Arts & Crafts, private inground heated pool with several decks. Enjoy a complimentary breakfast each morning.

The Grove Park Inn - 290 Macon Ave., Asheville, NC 28804 (704) 252-2711; (800) 438-5800. High Season (Summer-Dec.) Rates: $135-$425. Low Season Rates (Jan.-April) not yet published. Built in 1913 and furnished by the Roycrofters, it now has two huge wings and its capacity is 800 rooms. Complete with sport facilities and golf courses.

The Inn at Blue Stores - P.O. Box 99, Star Route, Hudson, NY 12534 (518) 537-4277. Rates $65-$165. Innkeeper: Linda Saulpaugh. Built in 1908 by Russell Foland as a gentleman's farm, it is a distinctive, Spanish Mission style-only a short distance (across the Hudson River) from Savoia's Auction House in S. Cairo, NY. CHO members.

The Orchid Tree Inn - 261 South Belardo Rd., Palm Springs, CA 92262-6386 (619) 327-2242; (800) 733-3435. Innkeepers, Karen and Bob Weithorn. Rates: July 5-August $90-$300; Low season rates not yet published. A California mission-style complex of buildings: from intimate studio to suites, from garden cottages and cabins to full-sized houses and bungalows, accommodations are casually inviting and lovingly maintained. CHO members.

The Palm House - 1216 Palm Ave., San Mateo, CA 94402 (415) 573-7256. Rates: $60-$80. Proprietors: Marion and Alan Brooks.

The Park Place Bed & Breakfast - 740 Park Place, Niagara Falls, NY 14301 (716) 282-4626; (800) 510-4626. Proprietors: Louise and Tom Yots. Rates $70-$80; CHO members.

The Pebble House - 15093 Lakeshore Rd., Lakeside, MI 49116 (616) 469-1416. Innkeepers Jean and Ed Lawrence. Rates: $90-$220. Delightful and deliberately decorated in Arts & Crafts to match the 1912 Lake resort. This B&B is well done with talent, care, signed and generic Arts & Crafts. Consider going out of your way for the inspiration. Enjoy the Scandinavian style breakfast served on the Roycroft China. Open thru Sept. 1997 .

The Queen Victoria - 102 Ocean St., Cape May, NJ 08204 (609) 884-8702. Innkeepers: Joan and Dane Wells. Rates: $90-$260 depending on room, day of the week and season. A Queen Anne with a fine Arts & Crafts collection in the public rooms. Their Christmas activities are wonderful! CHO members.

The Roycroft Inn - 40 S. Grove St., East Aurora, NY 14052 (716) 652-5552. Rates: $120-$210. Originally, at the turn-of-the-century, the Roycroft Inn was part of a Utopian Community dedicated to the Arts & Crafts ideology. All Fourteen of the Roycroft buildings are National Historic Landmarks. It is one of the foremost Arts and Crafts Era Inns in America. The Roycroft Shops are located across from the Inn on South Grove Street. CHO members.

Saint Joseph Inn - Formerly Snow Flake Motel. Inspired by Frank Lloyd Wright. 3822 Red Arrow Hwy., Saint Joseph, MI 49085 (616) 429-3261

Almost all of the National Parks and Adirondack Lodges were originally simpatico to the period in style, philosophy and activity. Those listed are sure to be restored or are in that process:

Sagamore Lodge - Sagamore Rd., Racquet Lake, NY 13436. Mid-week cross country skiing, snowshoe package weekend. Closed March/April and November/December. On the National Register of Historic Places. Non-Profit.

Timberline Lodge - Timberline Ski Area, OR 97028. Open 365 days a year. Totally handcrafted in 1930's, but truly Arts & Crafts with a WPA flavor furniture, linens, and architecture. High up on Mt. Hood! Skiing, hiking and a great view.

The Ahwahnee Hotel - in Yosemite National Park, CA 95389. Most rooms have woodburning fireplaces and deluxe furnishings, and some with kitchen facilities. It is a favorite of our many California members.

MacDonald Lake Lodge - Lake Macdonald, Montana 5992. In Glacier National Park, Montana and Canada. The Lodge dates from 1914 with Indian petroglyphs in the 3-story lobby with natural cedar logs. A must-see and stay.

Arts & Crafts Organizations and Societies

Western New York CHO Chapter
31 South Grove Street
East Aurora, NY 14052
(716) 652-3333
Fax: (716) 655-0862
Kitty Turgeon, Roycroft

Craftsman Farms Foundation
2352 Route 10
Parsippay, NJ 07950
(201) 540-1165

Friends of the Gamble House
Probably the oldest organization with the most spectacular Museum Arts and Crafts House as its focus.
4 Westmoreland Place
Pasadena, CA 91103-3593
(213) 681-6427

Foundation for the Study of the Arts & Crafts Movement
Kitty Turgeon, executive director
Robert Rust, curator
@ Roycroft FSACM
31 South Grove St.
East Aurora, NY 14052
Email: rycrft@aol.com
(716) 655-0562
Fax: (716) 652-3333

Pasadena Heritage
80 West Dayton Street
Pasadena, CA 91105
(818) 793-0617.

Frank Lloyd Wright Building Conservancy
343 S. Dearborn
Chicago, IL 60604
(312) 663-1786
Call to see if there is a local chapter near you for Frank Lloyd Wright owners, scholars and enthusiasts.
www.swcp.com/flw

Frank Lloyd Wright Foundation
FLW School of Architecture
FLW Archives
East - Spring Green, Wisconsin 53588-9304
(608) 588-2090
West - Scottsdale, Arizona 85261-4430
(602) 860-2700

Charles Rennie Mackintosh Society
Queen's Cross
870 Garscube Road
Glasgow, G20 7EL
Scotland
Telephone: 041-946-6600
Patricia Douglas, Exec. Director

Colorado A&C Society
Boettcher Mansion
900 Clorow Rd.
Golden, CO 80401
(303) 526-0855

A&C Society of CentraL NY
P.O. Box 82
Syracuse, NY 13210
(315) 463-1560

William Morris Society of England
Kelmscott House,
26 Upper Mall
Hammersmith, Longon W69TA
UK
Tel. 081-741-3735

William Morris Society of Canada
36 Tennis Crescent
Toronto, Ontario M4K 1J3
Canada

Arts & Crafts Omaha
(CHO Chapter)
8301 Davenport Street
Omaha, Nebraska 68114
(402) 391-2884
Jeannie Matthews, contact

Portland Arts & Crafts Society
(CHO Chapter)
The Handwerk Shop
8317 S.E. 13th Ave.
Portland, OR 97267
(503) 236-77870
Linda Willis, contact

American Pottery Association
Holds auctions, sales and conventions
Jean Oberkirsch
P.O. Box 525
Cedar Hill, MO 63016

Strangl/Fulper Collector's Club
P.O. Box 64
Changewater, NJ 07831
(908) 782-9631

Tile Heritage Foundation
Publishers "Flash Point," quarterly bulletin
P.O. Box 1850
Healdsburg, GA 95448
(707) 431-8453
Also publishes "Tile Heritage," Biannual Magazine

Graycliff Conservancy, Inc.
Dedicated to the preservation of FLW's Graycliff located in Angola, NY
P.O. Box 207
Amherst, NY 14226

INDEX

PHOTOGRAPHY CREDITS

PHOTOGRAPHY CREDITS